CONTENTS

INTRODUCTION

Why did we write this book?

Before I moved to China, the first book I bought was "Chinese Phrases For Dummies." Once I spoke a bit of Mandarin, I looked for books on how to do business in Asia.

There are a ton of books written about marketing, and almost as many about doing business in Asia. However, when I tried to find a practical guide that combines the two areas and can be applied to a growth scenario, I couldn't find a book that matched that criteria.

So I did what most people would do. I asked successful execs in the region if they could recommend such a book. But no one had an answer for me. This is why I decided to create a guide that would help answer people's burning questions about marketing and growing a business in Asia.

What will you learn from this book?

Firstly, let me clarify what this book is not—a quick guide to getting rich in Asia. This book is instead designed for people who are looking to build or grow a business over the long term.

Instead of simply sharing my experience in the region, I wanted to provide a broader view, which is why I interviewed hundreds of successful executives from different backgrounds and industries. They all had one thing in common —they were all people whom I wanted to personally learn from, as I felt that they have built or grown a successful business in Asia. So as you can guess by the title, this book features their success stories and case studies, along with a framework I created to bring it all together.

So if you're looking for a practical guide to marketing and growing your business in Asia, then this book is for you.

ABOUT THE AUTHORS

A 12-year Asia veteran known as "The Brand Builder," **Joe Escobedo** has presented to and trained over 7,000 executives from around the world, from startups to Fortune 500 firms, on building and managing their brands.

He was formerly a Forbes contributor covering digital marketing and PR in Asia and has contributed business insights to other top-tier media, such as Inc. and HuffPost. His articles have been viewed over a million times.

He was awarded the "Most Influential Global Marketing Leader" at the World Marketing Congress in 2017 and was rated the top speaker at the 2018 ASEAN CMO Conference.

Esteemed international companies, including Prudential, Scholastic, Arkadin, and RS Components, have sought his counsel.

Escobedo holds an MBA in international business and finance from the joint Oklahoma City University and Tianjin University of Finance and Economics program, as well as a bachelor's degree with honors from the University of Central Oklahoma.

Prethika Nair is a writer with a background in international relations. Her interests lie in political and socioeconomic developments in the Southeast Asian region. She has written articles for some of Asia's top brands including the Lee Kuan Yew School of Public Policy and Grab, among many others.

UNDERSTANDING ASIA AS A REGION

BY PRETHIKA NAIR

Asia is home to some of the fastest-growing economies in the world. The Asian Development Bank (ADB) estimated that the region's growth was 6% in 2018 and sets it at 5.8% in 2019[1].

Although Asia, as a region, is becoming more economically cohesive, many people outside of Asia think of the continent as one large market, which simply isn't true. There are huge cultural and economic differences across the region, and grouping such a diverse range of nations under one label would be an injustice.

However, don't be intimidated by this. By doing the right research and following some basic rules, you'll find the region a highly rewarding and dynamic place to do business.

In this book, we look at some important cultural norms and how you can navigate around them. Providing a comprehensive economic and social overview of Asia could constitute a book in itself, so we've summarized some key issues here. This list is by no means exhaustive, but we hope it helps to provide some context to the case studies that you will come across in later chapters.

The benefits of doing business in Asia

With Asia's rapid growth, needless to say, there are many benefits of doing business in the region. Here we look at some of the advantages of starting your own venture in Asia. As mentioned, the economic and political factors vary within the region, so these should be taken into account as well.

1. Relative ease of doing business

In the World Bank's most recent "Doing Business" report[2], three out of the five top economies for ease of doing business were in Asia. These were Singapore (ranked 2), Hong Kong (ranked 4) and South Korea (ranked 5). The report measures the various factors that affect a business from beginning to end, such as securing construction permits, ensuring electricity supply, registering property, access to credit, and enforcing contracts. Generally, most countries in the region are open to foreign investment and don't make it too difficult to set up a business.

Two of Asia's largest economies in particular, India and China, have made significant progress as of late. China, for example, has had notable improvements and is now among the top 50 economies in the world. This is thanks to various reforms to the economy, some of which include streamlining the process of obtaining a building permit and making electricity more accessible in Beijing and Shanghai by expanding network capacity.

India has also made significant improvements in the parameters of starting a business, such as dealing with construction permits, getting credit, and so on. Rita Ramalho, acting director of the World Bank's Global Indicators Group, says, "With three-quarters of regional economies making positive reforms, it's no surprise that this is a record year for regional reforms. India, as the largest economy in the region, is leading by example with its eight reforms."

Economic growth and a growing population also mean that Asia is seeing unprecedented levels of investment and development in infrastructure. Regional governments understand the need for expanding current infrastructure options, but there is a significant lack of funding. China is currently attempting to bridge the infrastructure gap with its Belt and Road Initiative, which aims to connect Asia, Africa, and Europe through continental roads and sea routes in order to improve trade flows. There are also many opportunities for external institutions in the private sector to also step in and fill in the gap.

That being said, however, some countries that ranked among the lowest in the World Bank's report on the ease of doing business were also located in Asia, such as Bangladesh (ranked 177), Myanmar (ranked 171), Laos (ranked 141), and Cambodia (ranked 135). Nevertheless, this doesn't mean that there aren't opportunities to be found in less developed countries. Ultimately, it comes down to which market best suits your intended business, as different countries provide different opportunities depending on the sector. We speak a bit more about this in due course.

2. Getting around

Just like Europe, traveling within the region is relatively uncomplicated and can be extremely affordable because of the proximity of countries to one another. Kuala Lumpur, for example, is a mere hour's flight away from Singapore, and many business travelers make this commute back and forth within a day.

Despite rising fuel costs, the demand for air travel in Asia is still predicted to grow steadily in the near future. Economic growth and a growing middle class have led to an abundance of budget airline and bus options between countries. The International Air Transport Association states that China is set to overtake the U.S. as the world's largest aviation market by 2030[3].

In Southeast Asia especially, leaders have realized the importance that transport plays in trade and tourism flows within the region. The member governments of the Association of Southeast Asian Nations (ASEAN), for instance, are constantly looking at ways to ease travel among the various countries, such as by signing agreements that would make travel by bus across countries much easier. Not only does this benefit ASEAN citizens, it also encourages investment opportunities due to the increased convenience of getting around.

However, this doesn't take into account local transport conditions. What would normally take 20 minutes can take up to 2 hours because of congestion in bigger cities such as Jakarta. Therefore, this is something that should also be considered in your search for the ideal market.

3. Tax havens

By OECD standards, tax systems in Asia can be more reasonable than those in Western economies. Singapore, for example, is extremely tax friendly and does not impose tax on specific overseas income, even if it is credited to a local bank account. It has one of the lowest corporate tax rates in the world, at just 17%.

Once again, this varies across the region. China's taxation system is more complicated and includes a dizzying range of customs on businesses and individuals, including income taxes (corporate income tax and individual income tax), turnover taxes (value-added tax, business tax, and consumption tax), taxes on property (land appreciation tax and real estate tax), as well as taxes such as stamp tax, among others.

However, other countries have recognized the importance of making the process easier to attract greater foreign investment. Countries such as the Philippines, Vietnam, and Brunei have improved their systems by streamlining the tax process or introducing online filing, making it much easier to pay taxes.

4. Digital media – a powerful tool to be harnessed

Regional economic growth also means increased access to technology across the region. Levels of information and communications technology (ICT) use may vary drastically between different countries, but stronger economies like Singapore and China are taking the lead in adopting key emerging technologies.

The number of internet users in Southeast Asia grew by more than 30% (or 80 million new users) between 2016 and 2017 alone. This means that more than half of the region's population is now online. For people exploring digital opportunities, Asia's increasing connectivity makes it an attractive destination. Therefore, harnessing the power of digital media is essential for the success of your venture.

Asians are incredibly tech-savvy and using these channels is very important. What this also means is that poor digital campaign integration can affect your credibility. Consumers trust in social media less and less due to poor content. The 2018 Edelman Trust Barometer[4] reports declining trust in social media. This is traced to what the authors call a "crisis of trust," namely, a loss of faith in institutions ranging from businesses to government and nongovernmental organizations. A major contributor, they believe, is the lack of objective facts and rational discourse, notably on social media.

How can marketers foster trust on these channels? We speak about this in due course.

Challenges of operating a business in Asia

Although the region's rapid economic growth makes it the prime location to conduct business, it doesn't come without its own challenges. This doesn't necessarily mean barriers to entry, however. All it takes is careful consideration of the unique conditions and cultural differences in order to navigate the landscape.

1. Mastering cultural and business etiquette

A simple Google search on 'business etiquette in Asia' turns up 10,100,000 results. The fact that so many guides have been written on the subject attests to its importance. The term itself tends to evoke notions of tedious procedures and attention to seemingly meaningless details, such as how to receive business cards or how to behave during a meal. In Asia, however, etiquette doesn't merely influence the way business is done. It *is* the way business is done, and could be the one thing preventing you from closing that all-important deal.

You'll see some examples of this aforementioned etiquette in the course of this book. What we've mentioned here are general observations and are merely meant to be a rough guide. The best way to learn is ultimately to spend some time in your host country to best understand the cultural nuances.

2. One size doesn't fit all

The Asian target market is vast. There is no such thing as 'one size fits all' when you have to appeal to target audiences over so many different cultures. Certain images, symbols or terms that may be acceptable in one country can be offensive in another. What you can do, however, is do a bit of research and follow a few common sense rules to avoid any marketing disasters that could stop your success in its tracks.

This seems painfully obvious, but it needs to be said: Do not piss off your target audience. Thanks to the internet, we're no strangers to brand fails across the world. We'll cover some of these embarrassing mistakes in our later chapters.

3. Corruption and compliance

Corruption may be one of the biggest obstacles to Asia's economic growth. Unfortunately, practices such as bribery, collusion, and cronyism remain prevalent in the Asia-Pacific region. Other than Singapore, most countries in Southeast Asia do not fare well in Transparency International's (TI) Global Corruption Perceptions Index[5], with a majority of countries falling within the bottom half of the index.

Why is this so? TI attributes it to an overall weakening of democratic institutions and political rights. In countries such as Vietnam, for example, there are still numerous reported instances of companies bribing officials in return for contracts. TI's report states that almost two-thirds of citizens have had to pay bribes in exchange for access to public services. Additionally, despite the government taking a strong approach to punishment, the lack of political rights raises questions about whether arrests are fair.

In Asia, gift-giving in the process of a negotiation is another tricky area. In Cambodia, for example, the custom of giving gifts is a cultural tradition in the country. However, this practice has extended into the realms of business and is even expected in many instances. A report by Transparency International Cambodia states that 66.3%[6] of businesses in the private sector had to pay bribes in order for things to get done.

The same wouldn't fly in Singapore or Hong Kong, both of which have strict anti-corruption and anti-bribery regulations. Ultimately, however, even if a country has regulations in place, without strong enforcement, corruption cannot be eradicated.

Another issue due to corruption is quality control. China, for example, has developed a reputation for its lack of quality control, although it has improved significantly in recent years, compared with a decade ago.

One way to navigate around this is to again understand the culture of your host country. In China, because relationships are so important, suppliers may not be upfront about delays or complications, just so they may avoid a confrontation. Therefore, it's important to be as clear as possible about what you expect from those you deal with.

4. Tensions and territorial tussles

It is important to understand the geopolitics of the region, as it could pose problems, depending on what sector you're involved in. Tensions still do exist in the region. The South China Sea dispute, for example, sees China, Vietnam, and other countries in the region laying claim to a group of islands. China, with its military prowess, has encroached significantly into these islands, and the other countries are alarmed. If conflict does arise, this could cause problems for trade between countries and flow of goods between borders.

Another facet to consider is the region's relations with the West. Tensions between China and the U.S. are relatively high, with either side imposing tariffs on the other for billions of dollars' worth of products. The U.S. has also criticized China's trade and intellectual property policies.

That being said, however, the region is relatively politically stable. Although there have been concerning developments in the past few years, these do not seem to have had a major effect on the economy. Thailand's military junta, for example, is still in power four years after its coup, but the Thai Baht has not suffered.

Asia is arguably the most dynamic region in the world now, with its rapid levels of development and its relatively stable political and economic situation. Everyone is looking to the region for expansion, and rightfully so, because of the immense potential it holds.

Factors to consider before launching or growing a business in Asia:

Determining objectives - What size of business are you looking at? Who is your target audience?

Willingness to adapt to local cultures - Are you willing to adapt to different cultures in Asia? Are you comfortable with long hours and being contactable 24/7?

Plans for geographic expansion - Will you focus on a specific market or region?

Working with local partners - How comfortable would you be delegating a share of your business to a local partner?

Financial goals - Does the host country provide support for SMEs and startups? Which countries are more conducive for your type of product or service?

CHAPTER 1:

THE T.R.U.S.T. SYSTEM

What if we told you there was a framework that could help you grow your business in Asia? What if we told you that this framework is so simple that it only has five key elements that could accelerate your company's growth and help set you up for success?

That was the intention in developing the T.R.U.S.T. system. It's a framework that's simple yet effective enough that anyone could implement it and see changes in their organization.

First, here's an overview of the system and the five key elements:

1. **T**rust
2. **R**elationships
3. **U**p-close
4. **S**hake-up
5. **T**alent

How did we come up with the T.R.U.S.T. system? Well, after interviewing hundreds of successful executives, founders, and teams, we identified these five common threads among most of them.

Now, it's important to keep in mind that each element alone may not be enough to drive change, but when you combine them in your organization, that's when the real magic happens.

Each chapter in this book is dedicated to a specific element and we'll be sharing real-life examples and case studies of how successful organizations and individuals have leveraged the T.R.U.S.T. system, and the results they've been able to achieve.

So if that sounds like something you'd be interested in, then keep reading, take notes, and, most importantly, apply the lessons you find valuable from this book.

This book alone will not make your business dreams come true. But if you implement the lessons in here and find success, then please let us know and hopefully we'll be able to feature you in the next book.

If for some reason, you don't learn one thing from this book, not one single thing, well, you can always use it as a decorative coaster.

Hope you enjoy!

CHAPTER 2: TRUST

BUILD TRUST, NOT A FOLLOWING

"All the world is made of faith, and trust, and pixie dust."

- J.M. Barrie, creator of Peter Pan

You might be wondering why we included 'trust' as both the name of the system and as one of the key elements. Well, among all the elements of the TRUST system, 'trust' is paramount because without building trust among your audiences first, the other aspects won't really matter.

The second thing you're probably thinking is: The word 'trust' gets thrown around a lot among business leaders and marketers, but what does it really mean? How can I go about gaining such trust? These are important questions that we will address in this chapter.

The new T&Cs (Trust and Credibility)

Let's consider what 'trust' means in the first place. Trust is the belief in the reliability of something or someone. In a business context, 'trust' means your audience's faith in whatever you're saying or offering, and them wholeheartedly believing that you will deliver on your promises.

Like other elements of the TRUST system, trust is not something you can build overnight.

For example, it took me at least five years to build my brand and build trust among my audiences. So anyone who says you can instill trust in your audience overnight is probably trying to sell you a pipedream or has never done it themselves.

Now, how did I get started building trust with my network? I began by creating valuable content for them and giving it away for free.

When you've worked hard on something, it can be hard to just give it away without compensation. The fact is, everyone has access to thousands of resources at the click of a mouse button. What makes your content more valuable than others? By allowing audiences to sample your best stuff for free, they can get a taste of what to expect, and you can prove yourself as an expert in your field. The point is to make them realize that if what they're seeing is already so good, imagine how awesome the paid stuff must be!

Your next question will probably be, "How much free content should I give away?" Time is money, and you need to make a living, after all. I've written over 200 articles, spoke at more than 30 events, and have written over 1,000 social posts with the hopes of providing as much value as possible to my audience. This is what helped to create trust in me.

Now, we're not saying that you have to produce that much content to build trust among your clients and prospects. We know folks who have only produced a dozen or so blog articles before finding success. The point is, you have to do what it takes to build that initial name for yourself. This creation of trust and a personal brand has not only done wonders for my business, it has also helped others build sustainable revenue generators.

Speaking to so many people has taught me one thing: People do business with other people, not businesses. One more time: People do business with other people, not businesses. So whether you're in B2C, B2B, or the public sector, your personal brand and trustworthiness are keys to your success.

As mentioned, proving your worth can take years, but we realize you're not reading this book to learn something that will benefit you a couple of years from now. You're looking for answers that can help you grow your brand starting tomorrow.

So with that in mind, we look at a powerful (and free!) tool that has helped business leaders supercharge their careers and businesses: online social networks, in particular LinkedIn.

We'll mainly focus on LinkedIn, as it's the most relevant network in the business context. Although the use of LinkedIn varies from country to country in Asia, the principles we've laid out here can be applied to any social network or similar contexts.

2.1 Building trust with the power of LinkedIn & online channels

So you have a LinkedIn profile, and you've added your recent company and job title. Now what?

For many executives, that's where they stop. But if you refrain from going further, you're actually missing out on plenty of opportunities to build trust and your personal brand, which in turn could lead to interviews, speaking opportunities, or connection requests from clients, employers, or partners.

Not to sound like a broken record, but building your brand can't be done in a day. If you're willing to put in the effort over time, you will reap the rewards. To help you get on the right track, here are some tips that will help you build a powerful personal and professional brand online.

1. Set specific goals so you know where you want to go

You can only assess your success once you've set clear and measurable goals for yourself. The same applies to your LinkedIn efforts. What exactly do you want to accomplish on LinkedIn, and how do your goals tie in with your organization and your personal brand?

Write down your objectives, specify how you'll achieve them, and track your progress. For example, you want to increase connections in your industry by 1,000 in 12 months. That breaks down to about 85 new contacts per month. Now, how are you going to achieve that?

Charles Brewer, the former CEO of DHL eCommerce, had two things in mind for his LinkedIn strategy. First, he had the opportunity to visit more than 110 countries and work around the world. This helped him develop a global perspective and network. Next, he wanted to make sure that everything he posts, shares, and comments on LinkedIn is unfiltered and genuine. (This, of course, requires you to check with HR or your compliance teams to find out what you can and can't say on social to avoid any possible repercussions.) Knowing what you want out of LinkedIn helps you figure out your next steps.

Another CEO who uses LinkedIn for talent search, business networking, and keeping a pulse on the global tech community is Anna Gong, CEO of Perx.

She also shares and educates the tech and business community with her findings and learnings on industry trends.

According to Gong: "Like anything you wish to be great at, you have to put in a lot of time, energy, and commitment to it. Because we're a startup, we have to work a lot harder! We don't have a big PR budget, so we have to rely on ourselves to build our brand through conferences, speaking engagements, and more importantly, sharing and contributing to various digital platforms."

2. Find out who your audience is and how you can help

Have a clear picture of who you are writing for by creating an audience persona, i.e., your target audience profile. Ask yourself: "What are their challenges? How can I help solve their problems?"

Sounds like common sense, right? But of the thousands of executives I've trained, only a small fraction could answer both questions. Needless to say, they had a head start on their competition.

Freelance content strategist Virginia Bautista, for example, has built a personal brand that has helped her generate $3,000 in business each month from LinkedIn alone.

Her advice? "Read conversations among your target audience. Join the conversations and ask questions. Go where your target audience is. If they're in Facebook groups, join those groups and be part of the conversations. If they're on LinkedIn, read their posts and engage with their content. These interactions with them will help you discover their pain points, and it will help you create content that resonates with them," says Bautista. In short, do some homework on your industry and learn about your audience.

For example, as Bautista's target audience are freelancers from the Philippines, she joined the Facebook groups Freelancing Philippines, Professional VAs, and Freelancers Hub Philippines. From these groups, she found out that most freelancers are concerned about the "race to the bottom" trend in bidding sites like Upwork. Those offering the lowest rates are getting most of the jobs, essentially making it tougher for everyone to charge an agreeable professional fee.

"These insights enabled me to write content that gives freelancers a better choice, which is to build their personal brand on LinkedIn," Bautista adds.

It's also important to find your niche. Once you've defined your audience, narrow them down. "My biggest mistake when I started publishing on LinkedIn was writing without a specific audience in mind," says Bautista.

So how can you find your niche? Bautista suggests two tips: target a particular industry and provide a solution that addresses your audience's needs.

She says, "As a freelancer for nearly 10 years, I chose to focus on the freelancing industry because I understand the issues freelancers go through. And since not so many Filipinos know how to use LinkedIn or aren't aware of what LinkedIn is, I thought I could teach freelancers how to use LinkedIn to thrive in the industry."

In your quest to build connections, the size of your network doesn't matter as much as the quality of your connections. So when it comes to building your network, focus on quality over quantity.

LinkedIn has an efficient search algorithm that allows you to find relevant connections. Look for these professionals, connect with them, and then engage with them. Your posts will get more organic clicks, views, likes, and shares.

Using LinkedIn's advanced search function to find the right professionals to connect with is easy. We'll help break it down for you:

1. Type in the job title or any keyword describing your target audience in the search panel. For example, if you want to target CEOs, type 'CEO' in the search box, then select 'People' on the categories below.
2. Refine your search by clicking on 'All Filters' at the top right-hand corner. This is a critical step. If you want quality connections, consider your target audience and your niche as you select the users you want to connect with. The results will only be those from within your network (first-, second-, third-degree connections plus other members of groups you're in).
3. Connect with the list of suggested professionals and customize each message when sending out your connection requests.

Bautista explains her approach: "What I used to do was type 'freelance' in the search box to find freelancers within my network. I then refined my search by country to find freelancers only from the Philippines and selected second- and third-degree connections. This search gave me around 35,000 freelancers from the Philippines. I sent them personalized messages with my connection requests and took it from there."

Bautista gives the example: "Hi Juaymah, my name is Virginia, a freelance writer for nearly 10 years. We're both members of the Facebook group Freelancing Philippines. I wish to add you to my professional network, and I hope to collaborate with you in the future. Thanks and have a great day!"

If you're new in your target industry, the easiest way to generate awareness and interest for your brand is to partner with influential and relevant people.

Bautista says: "I once sent a cold email to the founder of Freelancing Philippines. Her group has over 11,000 members, which I thought was a huge following. She sent me a response, let me join her Facebook group, and I was invited to be a guest in a live interview titled 'Facebook Live with LinkedIn Power User Virginia Bautista.' That led me to growing my own connections who regularly read what I write."

And obviously, be social. Engage with the people who took time to comment on and share your posts. Bautista shares an observation: "I've seen LinkedIn users with huge followings who don't engage with interactions on their posts or page."

It's called a social network for a reason. It's not polite to start a conversation then take yourself out and leave people to it.

Also, think before you like, comment, and share. Every action you take on LinkedIn contributes to your overall branding.

Gong says, "I try to prevent myself from giving too many opinions that could backfire. If I'm contributing, it's either an update that I wish to share or relevant insights that I believe will bring something to my network. You don't necessarily have to contribute for the sake of contributing. LinkedIn is great for me to just keep a pulse on the industry at times, and other times, I'm either recruiting or networking with industry folks."

3. Maximize different online channels and take the conversation offline

One good way to increase awareness of your brand is to reinforce your brand on other media and republish your content on other platforms.

Bautista says she republishes her articles on Social Media Today and Freelancers Union. She adds, "I get several connection requests from people who had read my articles on those two platforms."

Take advantage of offline events where you can further build awareness of your brand. Don't be afraid to promote your articles that you know could be of value to your target audience. Encourage them to connect with you and check out your articles on LinkedIn and other platforms.

Get creative with your social copy and write headlines like "Are You a Freelancer? Here's Why You Should Stop Acting Like One" that will entice them to click. Don't just self-promote. Build your brand by showering your audience with value.

As Brewer puts it, "It is about building your presence across multiple channels, and I work hard to represent myself and the organization across digital platforms. I also try to be as visible as possible in more traditional spaces, including events, conferences, and press."

(We'll speak a bit more about how to build relationships offline in subsequent chapters.)

4. Educate your audience by sharing helpful, original content

If you want to be trusted and taken seriously, your content has to be credible. Support your content with research, check the facts from multiple sources, and offer fresh ideas.

"I personally prefer publishing long-form articles on LinkedIn, as they allow me to provide more industry insight," says Bautista.

The drawback here is that long-form content (over 1,500 words) takes more time to produce. Still, if you're building a personal brand, writing long-form puts you in a position of authority. It takes skill and courage to make your ideas public, after all.

Bautista's tips when writing long-form:

1. Use bullet points to highlight your key points.
2. Make your story crisp and clear by removing unnecessary words.
3. Make your copy scannable.
4. Avoid jargon.
5. Use simple words.

Cherilyn Tan, CEO of Asia Law Network, says, "If you're known for one thing and you consistently produce content that is professional and relevant in that field, people are happy to be your followers. For example, at our company, we produce legal content that is easily digested by any executive. I also reach out and engage in conversations with people in legal tech in other parts of the world."

Your content also needs to be relevant to the context. If you're in Asia, use relatable images with Asian representation, instead of staged stock photos from the West. A good copywriter who can 'speak' for your brand would also greatly help to connect with your audience.

We've established that pushy, hard-selling content is no longer effective. Instead, focus on educating your audience. Blogs, webinars, infographics, free e-books, and newsletters are all means of building trust and credibility among your potential customers, as well as educating them about your business. By figuring out what your audience wants and needs to learn about, you can teach them those things.

If done well, not only will your audience be grateful to your brand and therefore return for more content, but you'll also gain authority as a thought leader in your field. Helping your audience in a way that increases their competency and makes your product or service more useful to them is a win-win for both sides.

Building an audience may take time, but once you've gained that audience, you won't have to keep paying for ads or use other awareness-building tactics. However, it's also important to not make the mistake of assuming your consumers are captive audiences. You have to keep engaging with them to retain their attention.

What to avoid when building your personal brand

Gong explains, "Digital connection is inevitably part of our lives whether you are an avid participant, observer, or are against it. Thus, factors such as not taking care of your public image, complacency, and fear of personal privacy being exposed, or social media not providing value or being a waste of time need to be overcome. Some CXOs don't realize how much their public image influences their customers' perception of their company and culture."

Take Elon Musk, for example. Initially, his humorous tweets portrayed him as the quirky billionaire that everyone could relate to. His honesty gained him a huge following, and for a while, this cult of personality was integral in raising Tesla's stock prices. This is an example of creating an online presence gone right.

It quickly went wrong, however, when Musk published various tweets that included declaring that he was taking Tesla private. Tesla's shares naturally dropped by as much as 8%. Gaining a reputation for being honest is one thing, but after you've gained a following, exercising a level of responsibility in what you publish is crucial in ensuring you don't lose your credibility.

Speaking of credibility, your viewers also expect some type of integrity in your profile. How much time you dedicate to your brand identity and integrity reflects how well connected you are to your employees, customers, and partner community. Sharing too many opinions instead of relevant insights is a common mistake.

In a world where your customers, partners, and peers are getting more socially savvy, it's a necessity for all leaders and senior executives to understand the advantages of social media and ultimately have a presence on social platforms. People are going to judge you based on how valuable your social currency is.

How to evaluate your brand's trustworthiness

People tend to prefer reputable branded products even if they may cost more. Asian consumers are becoming the most powerful economic force in the world, thanks to an expansion of the middle class across the region. Due to greater purchasing power, people can afford (pun intended) to be more discerning about what types of products they buy. A more reputable brand naturally has greater sales figures than a regular brand selling the same item at a lower price.

How then can you make your consumers trust you? In a nutshell, be genuine. Don't rig your reviews and make perfect ratings the priority. Sometimes a bad review can work out well for a company if complaints are politely resolved. We'll explain this further in a bit.

When trying to figure out where your brand currently stands in terms of credibility, ask yourself a few questions.

First, do you have genuine reviews from real customers? Consumers are more skeptical these days, thanks to hard selling and self-proclamations of being five-star rated. This has led to the rise of review sites like TripAdvisor and Glassdoor, which allow people to air their frustrations. These websites are incredibly important in making (and maintaining) a name for your brand.

Second, do you resolve complaints swiftly and amicably? There are bound to be unpleasant reviews left by disgruntled customers who, for whatever reason, had a bad experience. 99% of your feedback could be amazing, and all it takes is that one nasty review to mar your company's perfect image.

Time is of the essence when it comes to damage control here. Responding as soon as possible shows other customers that you have acknowledged the issue and are taking the steps to fix it.

It's also important to respond in a friendly manner. Perhaps it was just a misunderstanding and you didn't actually do anything wrong. On the inside, you might be cursing this customer for being unreasonable, but keeping things peaceful is the best way to go about addressing the issue. Getting overly defensive just reduces your credibility in the eyes of customers. So take a deep breath and consider the long-term consequences before posting that snarky (even if warranted) response.

Most companies stop there when it comes to dealing with customers. If you want to take things even further, there's one last step here that many people fail to do, and that's checking in on your previous customers. This can take up a fair amount of time, depending on the size of your customer base, but this extra personal touch ensures loyalty from old customers.

Some tips on leveraging your personal or company website:

Since branding is key, it's important to invest in your website. Make it the hub of all your personal branding and content marketing work. "Your website should not look and sound like a brochure though," says Patricia Mulles, who recently led regional content and services marketing, Southeast Asia, Oceania, and Taiwan for Samsung.

"Rather, a manifesto of values and the brand story, and a live record of (mostly positive) engagements with the brand, shared publicly. The product or service talk is almost an aside because customers can do most of the talking." This could be as simple as posting photos of branded events where participants are shown smiling and engaged, or a curated hashtag feed of customer usage or endorsements on Instagram. There should still, however, be a page on product or service info elegantly presented and with less salesy words.

Key takeaway: Your personal brand isn't going to be built overnight. It takes time, commitment, and dedication, but if you continuously share helpful content and add value to the conversation, you will build a personal brand that will benefit you in the long haul.

2.2 To create impactful content, get inside your audience's head

Up until this point, we've talked about building trust and awareness by building your personal brand. You must be thinking, "That's all great, but how does this translate into leads and sales for my business?" Once again, you're asking crucial questions that we will answer in this next section on how successful organizations have generated leads and sales from their brand and content.

One of the most important processes when trying to establish trust in customers is to identify what you're missing and improve. To do this, you have to ask questions.

According to Robbie Richards, professional speaker and search marketer, "Content marketing boils down to three things: knowing your ideal customer, where your ideal customer hangs out online, and which messages resonate with them at each stage of the funnel."

To know your ideal customer, Richards suggests that you "Look at industry forums and social media groups, poll existing customers, and speak with your frontline sales team. Getting answers doesn't have to be expensive or time-consuming."

To learn where your customers spend their time online, "Ask existing customers which channels they use to research and validate purchase decisions. Set up and track a multi-attribution funnel using Google Analytics to see which channels are assisting the goal conversion."

To find out which brand messaging works, "Perform an inventory of all your existing site content. Flag each asset—product and service pages, blog, case studies, demo pages—with funnel position and target persona."

Ensuring momentum is key. This is where the importance of communication comes in.

Tracey Wallace, senior content manager at BigCommerce, has helped grow the company blog's organic traffic by more than 300% YoY. She believes that "Good content marketing is a habit, not a one-hit wonder. It involves building great content day in and day out, tweaking, optimizing, talking to folks, helping others out."

Reinforcing Richard's advice on asking the right questions, Wallace also suggests doing extensive user research prior to writing content.

Here's how Wallace conducts her research:

- Carrying out surveys with their audience on a regular basis, or simply asking for their insight or advice on a specific topic.
- Tapping Slack (a cloud-based work collaboration hub) groups full of customers or just general successful e-commerce entrepreneurs, and asking questions or showing them content to get feedback and advice.
- Building close and personal relationships with about 20 of BigCommerce's most successful entrepreneurs.
- Emailing these entrepreneurs regularly (almost daily) and featuring them in nearly every single article she writes.

What makes your content share-worthy? Being relevant. Aashish Chopra, head of content marketing at ixigo.com, has produced branded posts on

Facebook which have garnered 40M views in a week, and has won various marketing awards in Asia.

Chopra shares, "Content must be made for low attention spans, responsive to tiny mobile screens, drive conversations, and prioritize storytelling over production value."

He also adds that "When your content is share-worthy, you beat the platforms at their own game, saving on distribution, making the message so powerful that everyone becomes a messenger spreading your content like wildfire."

Chopra recommends asking yourself: "Why would anyone share it?"

Over the past three years, Chopra has done tireless experiments and identified five categories of share-worthy content, in which every option is backed by millions of organic views:

1. **Inspirational**: Inspirational content tends to be the toughest to produce, but it garners the biggest success.
2. **Useful**: After understanding what problems users face, one should find ways to creatively solve them. In this instance, the solutions are presented in a video format. This makes it easier for the audience to share the content with their friends who may be facing similar issues.
3. **Celebrate their life**: If certain pain points cannot be solved, relatable content is created instead.
4. **Topical**: Creating content that is based on cudrrent affairs and global news. This also provides users with a vehicle to share their own views.
5. **Change the world**: Content can create a genuine impact in the world. Acts of kindness can be celebrated, and the audience can become messengers of that particular idea. The brand hence becomes a conduit in promoting positive change.

"Remember, views can be bought, but shares are earned, and when shares start snowballing, that's when magic happens," says Chopra.

Key takeaway: Before you start developing any content, make sure you know exactly who your audience is, what messages resonate with them and, most importantly, how your content can add value to their lives.

If you can answer all those questions upfront, then everything else, including content angles and targeted keywords, becomes so much easier!

2.3 Managing a PR crisis

Thanks to social media, brand fails are documented on a daily basis. Remember when a Tesco in London featured an aisle display of Smokey Bacon Flavour Pringles chips for Ramadan? Or in Singapore, when Japanese restaurant Maki-San received criticism for calling its latest chicken sushi roll the "Maki-Kita," based off the opening words of the country's national anthem. However, the pun actually translates to "Curse us" in Malay.

Another thing about the internet? It never forgets. Italian luxury brand Dolce & Gabbana fell from grace when an Instagram video of owner Stefano Gabbana describing China as a "country of s***" surfaced. The subsequent wrath and extensive boycotts of the brand resulted in both owners of the brand apologizing on video. However, the apology wasn't taken too seriously because it wasn't the first time that the brand had made fun of the Chinese. A previous advertising campaign showed a Chinese model eating pizza and cannoli with chopsticks, as the stereotype goes. No matter how hard a brand tries to erase its mistakes, there will always be evidence of it on the internet.

These embarrassing mistakes are by no means reserved to smaller brands. Big companies make them too. In 2014, Ogilvy ran an ad for Kurl-on mattresses featuring Malala Yousafzai. What do the youngest ever Nobel Prize laureate and mattresses have in common? The ad showed a cartoon version of Yousafzai being shot in the head by the Taliban (which really happened), and depictions of her recovering and eventually winning an award for her activism. During her recovery process, she falls on a Kurl-on mattress and "bounces back." Are you cringing yet?

Ever wonder why when something goes wrong, you often hear the company spokesperson say something like, "We are investigating the matter, and we will update you shortly"? It's no secret that these replies usually come from pre-drafted and pre-approved templates.

When a crisis hits, the PR team plucks out the most appropriate template, tweaks it to the situation, and sends it to the media who are hungry for the scoop. While this may work with traditional media, social media users have less tolerance for meaningless template messages. Now that citizen journalism is a thing, the message you deliver really matters when there are tweets and YouTube videos of factory explosions, train wrecks, or burning phones.

So what can you do to bring the situation under control? Seasoned public relations practitioner Vanessa Seow provides her best tips for managing crises, based on her 16 years' experience protecting the world's largest brands. Before you can manage a crisis though, you first need to understand what constitutes a PR crisis in the first place.

When is it really a PR crisis?

Sometimes crises occur because of an accumulation of smaller issues that eventually become a disaster of global proportions. She cites the case of Samsung Note 7 phones combusting as an example of a major PR crisis.

"In the early days of the Samsung Note 7 self-combustible phone, it was not clear if it was a one-off product fault or otherwise," says Seow. "When a YouTube video of a burning phone went viral on social media, the mainstream media caught hold of it, and what followed was a series of unfortunate events that ended in a big financial write-off."

According to Seow, an online crisis becomes a PR crisis when firstly, there is an obvious loss of lives and properties, or environmental and reputational damage of a huge magnitude, such as a commercial airline crash. Secondly, if a negative video clip or photo is going viral online and is then picked up by mainstream media.

An angry customer posting a bad review on Facebook about unsatisfactory customer service is not a crisis. However, a YouTube video posted by a customer showing wriggling maggots in the food he just bought making it to the evening news—this is most definitely a crisis!

It's all in the delivery

In all these cases, companies should acknowledge the facts and keep it consistent, whether it is provided over social or mainstream media. Seow suggests that templates are good for when you need something to dish out when faced with an onslaught of journalists pushing microphones into your face for a statement. But what do you say on Twitter, Facebook, and the like when the factory continues burning in the background and netizens are busy snapping away?

Seow says that statements like, "We are investigating and will update you soon," sound robotic and clearly come from that said template. By contrast, "We hear you—we are working hard to solve this and promise to give an update," sounds more human.

Can you see the difference between the two?

Next, Seow speaks of the AirAsia QZ8501 crash in 2014. CEO Tony Fernandes tweeted within hours of receiving news of the missing airliner.

"In the subsequent days, he frequently tweeted, along with print media reports to support a consistent message. He communicated in an empathic and genuine manner. It made a huge impact on how the crisis rolled out under control," says Seow.

Freelance copywriter Megan Leung advises, "Use it as an opportunity to reach out and demonstrate that your business is run by compassionate humans. Just be mindful of your good-to-bad rating ratio and aim for 10:1."

In 2018, the unthinkable happened to Kentucky Fried Chicken (KFC)—they ran out of chicken. Hundreds of stores in the U.K. had to close when KFC ran into problems with its suppliers.

How do you save your reputation when you fail to deliver the one thing you're supposed to? You put up a full-page ad in the papers, with an apology explaining what happened. It read, "Huge apologies to our customers, especially those who traveled out of their way to find we were closed. And endless thanks to our KFC team members and our franchise partners for working tirelessly to improve the situation. It's been a hell of a week, but we're making progress, and every day more and more fresh chicken is being delivered to our restaurants. Thank you for bearing with us." No sugar-coating, no smoke and mirrors.

Sometimes it helps to be a bit tongue-in-cheek as well. Next to the ad was a picture of its iconic bucket, empty, but with the logo switched around to read "FCK"—yup, you read that right. Some people thought the ad was brilliant, and judging from the reception it received, it worked in KFC's favor.

In the case of the AirAsia QZ8501 crash, the CEO clearly stepped up. Especially when a crisis involves casualties and serious property or environmental damage, it's crucial for the person at the top to take control and responsibility. If the CEO is not available, the next in command should provide an update in the interim.

"This is, however, easier said than done," says Seow. It's not often that a CEO has a strong social presence. "When a spokesperson is lacking in active online presence, the company public pages should take over the communication role. The downside is that netizens are still facing a non human entity, and this may get them all fired up."

The recent case involving hackers bringing a halt to Singapore telecom player StarHub's services is a good example. It did not take long for more than 1,600 angry customers to take to their keyboard and air their grievances on the company's Facebook page. The CEO, Tan Tong Hai, did not seem to have an active social page and this just added to the ire of the customers.

Seow says, "Most companies forget that their front line of defense is actually their employees. In today's connected world, someone is bound to be a friend or family of an employee. Guess who they will turn to if they want to know the latest rumor? Ensure employees are kept updated of established facts and adhere to a code of conduct required during crises."

Where does the action happen?

Marketers complain that there are too many social networks now to keep track of. Fortunately for marketers, when an issue does indeed become a crisis, it usually takes place in public spaces, such as Facebook or Twitter, or is made viral by popular news sites that drive huge traffic.

"If the onslaught of negative customer comments started on Facebook, focus your efforts on driving the conversation there first, then address other comments from secondary channels, such as Twitter or LinkedIn," advises Seow. "If the negative news is made viral by news sites, focus on communicating with journalists to tell your side of the story."

Very often, companies use social media listening tools that notify them before something gets out of hand. Such tools will give you a good indication on how you can direct your budget and efforts towards damage control.

However, companies tend to be slow to react, and netizens then take their battlegrounds to where they can most effectively air their grievances. These are typically a company's Facebook page, Twitter profile, or Instagram account.

The post-crisis mop-up

When the dust settles, it's time to look back and repair the damage. Seow shares some tips you may want to consider:

1. Keep a log of every tweet, response, news, customer, and journalist whom you were in touch with during the incident. Make sure you keep in touch with the key influencers in this group. They will appreciate the follow-up and, in the long term, could even turn out to be positive advocates for your company.

2. Assess how you reacted. Was it timely? Was it done with a human tone? Update your crisis playbook with the latest workflow that has proven to work.

3. Review your crisis committee team and evaluate if there are other key figures or personnel who should be involved should another crisis occur. Also review your social media activity (or lack thereof) and the tools that helped you during the incident.

4. Practice, practice, practice! Just as the militaries around the world conduct simulation exercises regularly, so should organizations conduct simulated incidents to see how prepared they are to deal with them. Many PR firms and risk management consulting companies have proprietary software that helps you conduct a social media crisis simulation exercise covering different scenarios. Your team should be going through such exercises at least once a year.

Key takeaway: First, identify what constitutes a PR crisis. If you are indeed involved in a PR crisis, then immediately gather your team and spokesperson to determine the best course of action. Remember that people ideally want a swift answer from a person, not a faceless brand, so make sure that your spokesperson is able to convey empathy and speak in a "human" manner. And after the crisis ends, don't forget to document all of your actions taken, so you can learn from the situation and hopefully prevent it from happening again.

CHAPTER 3: RELATIONSHIPS

BUILD A NETWORK TO BUILD AN EMPIRE

"Personal relationships are the fertile soil from which all advancement, all success, all achievement in real life grows."

- Ben Stein

When I moved to Singapore, I found it incredibly hard to get a job. So difficult, in fact, that I faced deportation because I nearly wasn't able to get an employment visa in time. Thankfully, I secured a job a week before that would've happened.

So what led to my struggles? Partly, ignorance. I thought that my background working for one of the world's top communications firms and advising Fortune 500 firms would be enough to have employers lining up to hire me. That, unfortunately, wasn't the case.

So what was I missing? A network. When I moved to Singapore, I didn't know anyone. That meant no local references and no one that could refer me to positions. But I learned from my failures and vowed to build a strong network in Singapore and the surrounding region. Over the past five years, I've been fortunate to build relationships with some of the smartest and most powerful CEOs, marketers, and entrepreneurs in the region.

How did I go from not knowing anyone to amassing a network that has led to nearly every job and project I've secured since moving to Singapore? And more importantly, how can you build relationships that can catapult your career and brand?

If you want to build a strong network, remember just one thing from this chapter, and make sure it's this: give far more than you take.

What do I mean by "Give far more than you take"? Your intention when connecting with someone shouldn't be "What can I get from this person?" Instead, you should be asking yourself, "How can I help this person?" If you have that question in mind before every connection request, every meeting and every call, then you'll be on your way to building everlasting relationships.

I'll give you an example. I've spoken at the region's largest events over the past couple of years. The catch? I haven't pitched myself for anyone of them. I was either recommended by someone or invited by the organizer. How did this happen? It all boils down to one thing—I added value to that event producer first.

Think about it, many event organizers are inundated with requests from people saying things like, "Hey! I'm big stuff and you should put me on stage because…" Okay, maybe not that blunt, but that's essentially the message that comes across to the producer.

So how did I do things differently? I built relationships and added value to the right producers first. Instead of emailing them and saying something like the message above, I'd connect with them on LinkedIn and say something like, "Hey! Noticed you're managing the upcoming (insert event). I took a look at your website and social channels and have a few ideas on how you can build awareness and buzz for the event beforehand. Here are a few quick ways…"

See the difference? At no point did I say, I should be onstage at your event. Why? Because no one cares what I want, they only care about what they want. Let me repeat that: People only care about what they want. And event organizers want to sell as much as they can.

The same applies to how I've built my business. I haven't actively done any selling, yet I've been able to work with some of the world's most prestigious brands.

How did I do it? By providing so much value that they eventually feel inclined to team up with me. Think about it, while everyone else is trying to pitch their products or services to them, I take a different approach by sharing relevant resources and tips, which I feel could benefit them or their business. So who do you think they're going to choose to work with?

Remember, building relationships isn't just about making the contacts to land you opportunities, it's also having a strong desire to help others. As Dale Carnegie puts it in his book "How To Win Friends & Influence People": "The rare individual who unselfishly tries to serve others has an enormous advantage."

So are you ready to start understanding how to grow and cultivate relationships? Well, keep reading, as we share how some of the region's most successful leaders did it.

3.1 Building relationships like an introvert

Building relationships in Asia is slightly different from how you might do it in the West. Instead of going out drinking and meeting people at networking events, some tend to prefer building relationships one-on-one or in smaller groups. Why is this so? It comes down again to trust. In Asia, strong relationships are valued even in business contexts. One executive told me that he needed to meet prospects in Asia several times before a deal was closed. On the other hand, he told me he was able to close deals over a phone call or two with his prospects in the West.

How about if you're looking for new prospects or partners? Because of the potential facetime, events are still one way of building relationships. This, of course, requires small talk, which didn't come naturally to me. Despite having spoken onstage to more than 7,000 executives from around the world, I'm still terrified and awkward when it comes to engaging in small talk at events. Even giving an elevator pitch makes my skin crawl. That's why I've developed the "targeted networking" approach.

How does the targeted networking approach differ from traditional networking? Well, instead of meeting random people at events and other public functions, you're meeting with a person you have already built a rapport with. You know a bit about them so that getting to know each other is less of a painful, awkward process. More importantly, you know how you can help them. No uncomfortable silence, no more "Hi, my name is… And I do…" Doesn't that sound much better than the usual schmoozing that always seems to be required at business events?

So how exactly does the targeted network approach work?

Putting the targeted network approach in action for you

I've been able to meet some of the best and brightest minds from around the world—people who have very little time to spare. Mind you, these principles can apply to anyone. You don't have to have a fancy company behind you.

I've delivered over 30 public talks for free. Obviously, my primary objective was to provide value to the audience and therefore instill within them trust in me. But there's another powerful reason to start speaking at events. I'll give you a hint: The real magic takes place backstage, i.e., the speaker's lounge.

When you're speaking at the same event as people you admire, you're automatically placed on the same level as them—even if they are British royalty or, in my case, successful CEOs.

So how do I leverage public speaking opportunities? Well, after accepting a speaking engagement, I'll look at the fellow list of speakers and connect with them on LinkedIn and other social channels. Along with the connection request, I'll send a short message mentioning that we'll be speaking at the same event and how I look forward to meeting them.

Then if they accept my connection request, I'll see if there is an obvious way in which I can help them by reviewing their social profiles and any media they've been featured in. If there is, then I'll suggest we lock in some time for a quick meetup before or after their talk.

That way, I've already built rapport with them and know about them and how I can help. So by the time we do meet up at the event, it's like I already know them. No awkward intros and handshakes. We cut the small talk and go straight to how I could help them. Why is this so important? Remember, most of the people you're trying to build relationships with are time-starved and every second counts for them, so make sure you're making the most of their time.

From there, it's just about sharing how you could help them and sending them a follow-up email or text after the event to continue the conversation. That's the easy part. The hard part is getting them to spend their precious time talking with you, instead of other people at the event. Sounds easy enough, right? We know you might be saying: "Sounds great, but I'm not a public speaker and likely won't be doing any public speaking anytime soon. So how would this approach work for me?"

Well, firstly, if you're not doing public speaking already, then you should start now. There's no better way to add value and build trust and relationships with your audience. The reason for that is that people can see you, hear you, and interact with you. Plus, your credibility increases when you're asked to speak at prestigious industry events. But I understand that speaking in public is easier said than done. So let's say that you are just attending an event and want to connect with one of the speakers—where should you start?

The same logic applies, but instead of messaging them and saying that you're both speaking at the event, you become their unofficial speaker promotions manager. What do I mean by that?

Most speakers are so busy that they rarely have time to share or promote their upcoming talks. But that's where you come in. After you've already identified a speaker you'd like to meet at an event, you will share posts on social or your own channels promoting their talk. Mention how excited you are to hear their speech. (Make sure you tag the person, so they can be notified of your posts.) Take it one step further and create custom speaker profiles for social and share what you created with them. You don't need to be a designer, you can create one in under 15 minutes using a tool like Canva.

After you've gotten their attention, you can send them an invitation to connect on social. Then you can politely ask if they have 10-15 minutes to spare after their talk to listen to an idea or suggestion on how you can genuinely help them. (Note. This is not the time for you to hard-sell to them. It's the time to showcase your expertise and how you can add value to their lives.) Nine times out of ten, if you've gone through that much work already, the speaker will accept your invitation.

But let's say, for some reason, they don't see your message in time. You could always continue adding value by writing a blog post with your biggest takeaways from their talk, sharing it on social, and tagging them. They, or someone in their network, are bound to see it, and hopefully, they will feel obliged to speak with you after all the time and effort you've put in.

Sounds simple enough? Try it out and see what happens.

If you're looking for more practical ways to build relationships with your peers, clients, and prospects, then keep reading.

Key takeaway: Instead of gambling and hoping to find the right person to speak with at an event, do your research upfront and plan out who you want to connect with, even before the event. If you're a speaker, connect with your fellow speakers. If you're not a speaker, then make sure you add as much value to the person you'd like to chat with. That's the best way to get on their radar and get their time.

3.2 Building long-lasting relationships with the media to drive

sustainable awareness

We often think about building relationships with customers and partners. And while that is definitely important to growing your business in the region, it's also crucial that you forge relationships with other parties that could make or break your business. We're talking about the media.

We're not advocating going out and hiring a big-name public relations (PR) agency to manage your media relations. In fact, with the right strategies, you could bypass an agency, save thousands of dollars, and build relationships with the media yourself.

Sounds impossible? It's not, says Andrew Prasatya, head of content marketing (Southeast Asia) at iPrice group. According to Prasatya, he has a proven PR system that has helped his company get over 200 pieces of press coverage in Southeast Asia's top-tier media, without having to pay anything!

Prasatya shares some strategies you can use to get press coverage for your company.

1. Listing the top media outlets in your region

The iPrice group started their PR process by listing the top 50 media outlets where they operated: Indonesia, Malaysia, Singapore, Thailand, Vietnam, the Philippines, and Hong Kong. Afterwards, they set internal targets for the number of media articles they would secure in those outlets each quarter.

2. Building a relationship with the "right" journalist

After compiling the top media in their market, the team identified who would be the best journalists or editors to contact. Prasatya explains, "We spend our time and energy getting in touch with the right person at each media outlet. Since we're an e-commerce company, we look for writers who cover startups, e-commerce, and technology."

Prasatya explains how his team builds solid relationships with the media:

First, they find the journalist's or editor's contact information via social media (LinkedIn, Facebook, Twitter) and invite them to connect. The iPrice team then reads their articles to understand what kind of topics and formats they like, as well as their writing style. Once they have their personal email, the team emails the journalist to explain what they like about their writing, give a brief introduction about iPrice, and share what story or research they're working on.

Since the iPrice team is based in Malaysia, they often fly to other countries for face-to-face meetings with journalists or editors. Sometimes they collaborate on projects together. For example, the iPrice team developed a blog post with tips on how Indonesian startups can build relationships with the local media. In this article, they featured videos of writers at well-known publications sharing their advice.

Once they have built rapport with the journalists, the iPrice team keeps in touch with them on social media. Prasatya sums it up perfectly, "A good relationship with the media is sustainable and mutually beneficial; not a purely transactional one."

3. Creating content that appeals to their audience (and yours)

The iPrice content marketing team then focuses on creating insightful and newsworthy content. "We will never only talk about how good we are, what service we offer, and other boring things," says Prasatya.

Some of the following examples of Prasatya's team's content were featured in more than 15 top news outlets across Southeast Asia and garnered over 5,000 social shares each:

1. Who in Southeast Asia pays the most for an iPhone 7? (Tech In Asia)
2. Garena Rebrands as "Sea," Secures $550M to Double Down on Indonesian E-Commerce (Inc.)
3. Why Grab is a cheaper option in Singapore (Singapore Business Review)
4. Did you fall for these? April Fool's 2017 best pranks and fake news (Channel NewsAsia)

How does iPrice create insightful and interesting content?

The team conducts research on what's gaining traction in Southeast Asia and around the world. To do so, they use online tools such as Google Trends, event calendars, local news websites, and good ol' fashioned talking to people.

Next, the team tries to create a unique story to capitalize on the momentum of a specific event. For example, the team saw a lot of media publishing uninspiring news about the iPhone 7, such as the evolution of the iPhone and the technology inside the iPhone. Seeing how boring this would be to the average potential consumer, they came up with a new approach, by deciding to rank countries based on the price of the phone in that country. They also compared how much people need to work in each country to afford the iPhone 7.

Finally, the team repackaged the article into different forms of content including an infographic, interactive content, and video.

4. Testing, analyzing, and optimizing your media pitch

After the content is ready, the team presents their media pitch. Before sending their pitch, the team gets in touch with the right person in the media, depending on the type of story.

Prasatya says: "We always do A/B testing with our approach to the media to see which approach is better. For example, we try many different formats and track the response rate and conversion or publication rates. Then we will use the one with the highest response and conversion rates."

5. Sharing the love on social

Whenever a journalist publishes one of their articles, the iPrice team always thanks them on social media and tags their personal and company social media accounts.

The iPrice team analyzed online consumer behavior during Ramadan in Indonesia and Malaysia. (Both Indonesia and Malaysia have the largest Muslim populations in Southeast Asia.) The team then compared 800,000 visits on their Indonesia and Malaysia websites, from two weeks before

Ramadan and in the first two weeks of Ramadan.

They found that people are using their sahur time (eating early in the morning) to shop online. In fact, they witnessed a 400% jump in online shopping during the Ramadan period. They also found that during lunch time, people use their lunch break to shop online—a 60% jump during the Ramadan period.

In Indonesia, the team pitched the story to the media, which got picked up by 15 top-tier media outlets including CNN. As a result, they received 10 quality backlinks.

In Malaysia, they pitched the story and it was featured in two popular local newspapers, online radio stations, and a TV interview.

As shown by the team at iPrice group, it's possible to successfully do your own PR if you follow these five key steps.

Key takeaway: If you want to build relationships with the media (or anyone else for that matter), you have to think of what's in it for them or their audience. No one cares about what your news is. Journalists (at least the good ones) only care about their audience and pleasing them. So have that question in mind when developing and pitching your content.

More importantly, think of building relationships with the media like you would approach dating and eventually marriage, rather than a one-night stand. That means, if a journalist features your piece, don't forget to thank them afterwards and continue to stay in touch by sharing valuable story ideas (even if they aren't yours).

3.3 Creating memorable experiences to build customer loyalty

The food and beverage industry in Asia is arguably one of the most competitive. On nearly every corner of the continent, you can find some amazing food options to choose from. So how do you stand out from the pack and win loyal customers? The answer: By creating memorable experiences.

The owners of the widely lauded restaurant Palms L.A. Kitchen and Bar, Christian Jensen and Michael Tsai, share how they developed a hotspot for anyone looking to take a break from Beijing's hustle and escape to

California, if only for an hour or two. "California means sunshine and lifestyle. Palms brings the relaxed-yet-sophisticated, youthful, and eclectic vibe of the L.A. dining experience to China," explains Jensen.

The duo were keen to avoid the common mistake of being a "brand first, restaurant second." Food is king. Jensen says, "The foundation of our business is pretty simple: flavor, service, and value. Our customers know they'll have a good time, and that they can afford to come whenever they want."

Keeping it real, the Cali way

The owners believe the restaurant has been successful because they have cultivated friendships among expats from the U.S. West Coast. These "Palms ambassadors" play a crucial role in promoting the restaurant on their social media channels. For this inner circle, "you can't fake it," says Tsai.

He adds: "In this age of instant reviews, we're completely dependent on our core fans. They build our brand and promote us without our even asking. We are completely transparent with them and stay in contact with them daily."

Among the "Palms ambassadors" are the L.A. Times' Beijing bureau chief and L.A. Tourism Board's China representative. Thanks to them, "L.A. Mayor Eric Garcetti and most of the City Council surprised us one night during an official visit—so we can also count fans in high places!" says Jensen.

Building an experience around your customers

Fellow F&B entrepreneur Matthew Slack, CEO of The Pizza Factory in Guangzhou, China, built his business by putting his customers at the heart of the restaurant experience. As a result, he was able to generate plenty of organic business from his happy customers.

His restaurant currently ranks No. 1 out of 4,212 western restaurants on China's most popular restaurant review app, Dianping. Like Yelp, Dianping allows users to sort restaurants by cuisine, with the highly ranked restaurants displayed at the top. It's like Google where if you aren't on the first page of search results, then you might as well not exist.

Slack says Dianping has been his restaurant's biggest success when it comes to attracting new customers. "About 60% of our business comes from customers who find us through the app and then rate us after finishing their dining experience," says Slack. So how did The Pizza Factory outrank over 4,000 restaurants in only two months?

Ask and you shall receive

While some companies buy fake reviews, Slack says his team would never resort to such shady practices. Instead, he advocates the rule of reciprocity, which is a social psychology term that explains your willingness to return a favor. In Slack's case, that is to help spread a positive word once you've had a positive experience.

"As a growing brand, we don't spend millions on advertising," says Slack. "We need word of mouth, and there is no better word of mouth than on restaurant review apps. Our pizza is great, but I don't rely on people who love the brand to go spread the word. We train our team to create a positive and unique experience that customers will want to share with friends and then ask them to spread the word."

Slack explains, "Checking on every table to ensure they are enjoying their food is not a common practice in China, but we're doing it within two minutes of food being served. It's so simple, but no one does it here."

"We're also constantly looking for ways to exceed expectations like giving free cookies or other small freebies. At the end of the meal if we felt they enjoyed themselves, we just ask for a small favor in return. We tell them, 'If you had a good time tonight, please leave some positive comments on Dianping.' They're usually happy to do so, and that's been the secret to us beating over 4,000 other restaurants, including industry titans like Pizza Hut, in less than two months after opening," says Slack.

He adds: "That's the great thing about social media and digital marketing. It doesn't matter how big your brand is or how much money you spend on marketing. If you can build a better customer experience than your competitors, people will notice and share online. Before sites like Dianping (or Yelp for that matter) came along, small brands like ours couldn't easily be found."

Scaling the customer experience across the region

Creating an exceptional customer experience is tough enough at one location, but how do you go about replicating that same experience across multiple locations and countries?

Steen Puggaard, the former CEO of <u>4FINGERS Crispy Chicken</u>, shares how he grew 4FINGERS from one outlet store to 21 in four short years. In doing so, he grew the company from $2M to a $30M business, from owned outlets excluding franchises.

"We put a lot of thought into what our brand stands for, connecting with our customers for the full brand experience, from their meals to the music played in-store. For example, we created a 4FINGERS Spotify playlist that connects consumers across all the countries we're present in. All tracks in the playlist were curated by the team. We also recently had an online game named Get Clucky. Customers received a special code with each purchase, and they could go online for a chance to win a 5-star trip to Melbourne. This contest helped us boost site traffic by 30% and collect a good amount of leads for future activities," says Puggaard.

He adds: "Rather than be seen as just a chain serving fried chicken, we wanted to give our customers the experience of casual dining in a vibrant, underground setting. We're about giving our consumers quality, tasty food that's against the norm. Everything about us reflects this—from our stores' designs with the graffiti walls and subway signs, to the grungy underground look of our website, down to our packaging. This all reflects the rebellion and disruption against the norm that we at 4FINGERS stand so firmly for."

Remember, there are two kinds of companies: those that develop products or services, and those that offer experiences. Think Starbucks. As Taha Bouqdib, president and CEO co-founder of TWG Tea, says: "Aim to deliver an experience that makes customers feel special at a cost that remains accessible. Hitting that sweet spot is what's good for business."

A large part of TWG Tea's success boils down to its world-class customer service no matter which outlet around the world you go to. That's why Bouqdib and co-founder Maranda Barnes place such a strong emphasis on training staff. For example, the team developed a comprehensive mobile app that functions as an internal training tool, a TWG Tea Book detailing information on the company's teas, accessories, and products.

When you dine at a TWG Tea outlet, you'll feel like a millionaire even if you're spending less than $100 for the whole meal. Or as Bouqdib puts it: "You will receive the same service, gift wrap, and silk ribbon for a $20 TWG Tea than if you had spent $200 or $2,000."

Key takeaway: Instead of getting bogged down worrying about which digital marketing channel you should invest in, first think about how you can create an exceptional customer experience. As highlighted above, happy customers can be your best source of promotion (and, of course, long-term revenue.) So when you're building your company, put their wants and needs at the very heart of your business strategy.

CHAPTER 4: UP-CLOSE

THINK PEOPLE, NOT COUNTRIES

"When people talk, listen completely. Most people never listen."

- Ernest Hemingway

So far, we've talked about the importance of building trust and relationships with your audiences. Now, let's take things one step further by really getting up-close with them. No, we're not referring to wiretapping your customers or resorting to shady data mining practices (hello, Cambridge Analytica). What we're saying is that many marketers in Asia think in terms of regional or local plans.

But many of them will tell you that you can't take a one-size-fits-all approach to marketing in Asia. Yes, you can have an overarching strategy of what you'd like to achieve in the region, but you still need to have an Up-close approach.

What do we mean by having an Up-close approach in the first place? Well, for example, many marketers in the region shout about the importance of localization. However, what does localization even mean?

For businesses entering Asian markets, consumer wants in the region may be somewhat of a puzzle. Varying demographics, levels of access to technology, and cultural differences are all things to consider.

Millennials, for example, make up a huge portion of consumer markets and are a very important target group. However, Millennials in Asia may not be the same as their Western counterparts. For example, familial relationships in Asia can affect an individual's buying decisions much more than peer pressure.

Many businesses entering the market tend to have something like a "China plan," for example. But anyone who has done business in China will tell you that you have to break China down into smaller, more manageable pieces.

To illustrate, when I was developing regional communication plans for a luxury automotive brand operating in China, we broke down the country into five regions: North, South, East, West, and Central.

The North comprised major cities like Beijing. The South included tech hubs like Shenzhen. The East consisted of Shanghai and the surrounding provinces. The Central comprised emerging markets like Chengdu and Chongqing. And in the West, to a lesser extent, we were focusing on any markets that had potential in the future, such as Yunnan.

Why did we split China into different regions? Because we realized that the languages, culture, and external conditions like weather vary greatly among regions. And because we were looking after the whole Chinese market, the regional breakdown was a start. If we were, however, managing a dealership in Beijing, we'd have to take a more Up-close approach, which means breaking Beijing up into districts and the people that populate that area.

The same applies to smaller countries like Singapore. It doesn't really make sense to create a nationwide "Singapore" marketing plan without understanding the economic and cultural differences that exist not from city to city but from neighborhood to neighborhood. And while this can seem a bit daunting, we will be sharing some real-life examples and tips of how successful organizations have gotten up-close and personal with their audiences.

4.1 Understanding and respecting cultural sensitivities

Before we delve into individual case studies, it is important to think about how running a business in Asia first requires a solid understanding of cultural quirks in the region.

The Asian target market is vast. There is no such thing as 'one size fits all' when you have to appeal to target audiences over so many different cultures. What you can do, however, is follow a few common sense rules to avoid any marketing disasters that could stop your success in its tracks. The brand fails that we've brought up in earlier chapters highlight the importance of understanding your audience. So, how can you go about doing this? Here are some tips:

1. **Express yourself in the target language**. Language can be a huge source of misunderstanding. Consider different dialects, with different nuances. In China alone, there are over 200 dialects, and in India, an estimated 720! Figure out whether the customers prefer more emotional or rational approaches. Get professional translators if you need to. But there's no substitute for buckling down and learning your host country's language. Doing so will not only teach you a lot about their culture, but it will also go a long way in showcasing your respect for them and their customs.

2. **Be sensitive about norms (and conversely, stereotypes)**. Here lies the importance of working with someone who has local knowledge and experience of local cultures. Too often people enter, stay, and leave a country without ever having really delved into the local way of life. It's a wasted opportunity to learn new things and truly understand what your consumers want. Also, it's important to investigate the taboos pertaining to a certain culture. We've already highlighted the embarrassing ways things can go wrong if you don't check for what can fly and what can't.

3. **Pay attention to the visual factor**. An image or scenario can be interpreted differently by various people. The idea of death may often be represented by the color black in Western culture, but in Asian countries such as China and Korea, white represents death. Imagery is so important—don't use a picture of noodles when talking about a rice dish, for example (and yes, that happened with a Yellow Pages ad in Toronto).

Now, just because you have to be careful with your imagery doesn't mean you have to be boring. If you've lived in Asia and you were asked to think about some of the best advertisements you've seen, there's one country in particular that would probably come to mind: Thailand. If you haven't seen Thai ads before, do yourself a favour and look them up online.

There seems to be a distinct formula to their ads. Create an engrossing storyline, make it emotional or funny, and only reveal the product towards the end. It's often weird, but it works.

In the subsequent sections, we'll share some real-life examples of how companies are avoiding cultural faux pas and getting up-close with consumers to grow their business.

Key takeaway: Take the time to thoroughly understand the culture of your host country to avoid offending anyone. The best way to do this? Spend some time in your host country or consult a local partner before launching any external communications.

4.2 Expanding in the region by hitting the ground

Online ads are dead, right? Tell that to Kosuke Sogo. His company, AdAsia Holdings, has expanded into nine countries and generated over $12.9 million in revenue in only eight months. They doubled that figure the following year to $26 million and grew their presence to 11 markets in Asia. On top of that, the company received $14.5 million in Series A funding, the most for an ad tech company in Southeast Asia. In January 2018, the company expanded into AnyMind Group, launched into Malaysia and the Philippines, and moved into the human resource industry, while closing its Series B funding round at $13.4 million.

How did Sogo achieve this tremendous expansion? Even before the company had been launched in April 2016, Sogo and his co-founder had already developed a strategy for overseas expansion. The idea of expansion is one thing, but to actually do it and perform well is a whole other beast. Therefore, they came up with three scalable pillars that have set the foundation for the company: people, innovation, and localization.

As explained by Sogo, bringing the right people in is paramount to a startup's growth, particularly in the early days. Age should not be an issue here, but rather, whether they have the personality and character to fit in and do well in the company.

Innovation is key to being competitive in this region, but being agile is even more important. Having the ability to quickly evolve and shift is the reason why they decided to start their own company.

This brings us to the third pillar. With Asia being such a diverse region, it is important to approach expansion with localization in mind. Each market in Asia has its own unique cultural norms and nuances. Strategizing ways to localize products, services, and manpower should be one of the first things to do when planning business expansion. This includes researching and understanding local business and industry practices, government grants and regulations, as well as historical market reception to products.

Bringing in local staff is a given, but an important aspect is to localize solutions as well. Take Thailand for example, users are almost equally on social media apps (Facebook, LINE, etc.) as they are on browsers. This has also become an essential part of Thailand's media consumption—social media has become their news feed. Thus, apart from obtaining desktop and mobile web ad inventory, AdAsia's publisher team also sourced local mobile and social in-app ad inventory to cater to this market.

Having covered the majority of Southeast Asian markets, the Greater China region, and Japan, AdAsia then looked into moving into Malaysia, the Philippines, India, Russia, and the United Arab Emirates.

Their experience in these countries revealed that quick and agile engineering teams are needed—with some working on enhancing existing products and some developing new solutions. This gives businesses the flexibility to quickly localize their products before entering a new market, while developing new solutions. For example, markets like India and Russia have sprouted their own ad tech and martech ecosystems, and businesses would have to partner up and integrate with local players to keep the momentum going.

On the marketing front, AdAsia aimed to employ a range of B2B and B2C marketing tactics when they entered markets. They shared with us some of the ways they aimed to reach target demographics for new markets.

On the offline end, trade shows are a must to get "face time" with prospective B2B clients and run product demos. There are many trade shows that have packages for interesting startups. Two things here that are required of staff: Wear the company t-shirt and hustle. There are other ways to stand out, of course, but first, find out what makes your company attractive.

AdAsia's reach in Asia attracted many potential clients and partners, especially those from the West looking to break into Asia—and their backdrop, brochures, and pull-up banners made sure of it.

Another way is to always be ready for product demos. If you have a booth, bring more than the required number of laptops needed, as your staff will be able to grab one to run the demo outside of the booth. Throw on a company t-shirt and you're pretty much a mobile booth.

Speaking of online, their key focus areas are organic and paid search, as well as influencer marketing. Google, Baidu, or whatever local search engine is usually the first place many people go to before making a purchase decision. Just getting into the conversation matters, even if they search for more information about a competitor. It then comes down to how your online properties can convert them.

AdAsia's future solutions in other industries also require a certain degree of B2C marketing targeted at digitally savvy users—and that's where influencer marketing comes in.

Most of the countries they're looking to expand into have high social media usage, and influencer marketing allows them to influence that precise audience. Of course, the message for each market has to be altered accordingly.

Why do some companies fail at expansion?

As Sogo says, "If you fail to plan, you plan to fail." He explains that as a startup, they knew that expansion would be tough at the start, but it was a unique stage of growth for advertising and marketing in Asia. That's why they decided to plan for quick expansion. Timing is key, and it's important that companies see the opportunity, plan, and act quickly.

Sogo and his co-founder had experience in this industry across the region and knew from the start that they wanted to set up the company in Singapore. They then planned to expand into Southeast Asia before moving into Greater China and Japan. Their industry experience helped them identify emerging, high-potential markets to expand into like Vietnam and Indonesia, which were just on the cusp of the growth we're seeing today.

At the same time, it is important to be dedicated, flexible, and always willing to learn and try out new things in Asia. For the first year of operations, Sogo and his co-founder flew around the region meeting likely candidates and potential clients, setting up offices and more, while overseeing operations. They even flew to as many as four countries within a week, often taking red-eye flights. This constant interaction with their customers meant that they could adapt their products and strategy to meet their needs.

That's not to say that their pace of work has changed since then. Their newer markets like Hong Kong, China, and Japan require more of a focus, and they still have to maintain the growth of their existing markets.

Again, it comes down to localization. Having a scalable plan and business is still very important, but keep localization top priority as well. Get your feet on the ground before expanding into those markets. Network with the locals, find out their pain points, and see how you can tailor your solutions to meet their unique needs. Sogo explains how, for example, marketers in Vietnam prefer to use managed marketing and advertising services, rather than self-service ad tech and martech platforms.

Apart from the technology that AdAsia offers to their clients, they've also built a team in Vietnam that consists of account and client support teams, similar to an agency. Additionally, they'll be looking to launch their free educational initiative there to upskill Vietnamese marketers. Remember, you have to cater to what the market needs.

For Western-based companies who want to expand into Asia, Sogo says, localization should play a key part in a company's expansion in the region. As we've mentioned, though, it's important to first understand that each country and even city has its own unique culture and characteristics. After researching the market and finding out whether there is a localized product fit, adopt a customized marketing, product, and operations strategy, and you will be able to see the benefits of this approach.

Find out if different cities in each market have different ecosystems as well. When AdAsia opened their office in Ho Chi Minh City, for example, it was only a matter of time that they had to open an office in Hanoi. "This is not due to geographical reasons, but more because Ho Chi Minh City has a generally higher level of digital marketing sophistication compared with Hanoi," says Sogo. Couple this with Hanoi consisting of mostly local businesses and government organizations, and a more consultative approach has to be used in sales.

Key takeaway: Before expanding into a new market, it helps to spend some facetime with your prospects, customers, and partners. Only by doing so will you understand the types of products or services, teams, and other pieces necessary to cater to them.

4.3 Boosting customer loyalty by mingling with customers

Southeast Asia's e-commerce space is booming. According to Frost & Sullivan, Southeast Asia is set to become one of the world's fastest-growing regions for e-commerce revenues, exceeding $25 billion by 2020. With that fast growth comes increased competition, which means only the best performing e-commerce platforms will survive. So what can you do to ensure that your brand thrives despite intense competition?

Many business owners tend to face similar problems when it comes to online conversions, such as ensuring that customers go through with the purchase of a product. Irwan Juanda is the former head of E-commerce at Damn! I Love Indonesia (DILI), a popular online clothing shop in Indonesia that has grown its year-on-year sales by 21%. He has shared with us the three main challenges when it comes to online conversions and customer loyalty, and what you can do to solve them.

Ensuring high conversion rates

Often, businesses embark on campaigns or promotions to boost sales but don't see the results in online sales. According to the company's initial in-store surveys, 70%-80% of the Damn! I Love Indonesia's customers were unlikely to purchase from their online shop. So how did they get offline customers to purchase online?

The answer lay in using Offline-to-Online (O2O) e-vouchers to achieve 90% conversions rates. The company did this by first placing promotional materials at all physical outlets to raise awareness about the e-voucher offer. These materials included standing banners, signage by the cashiers, and window displays. Sales staff were also trained to introduce the offer and the company's online shop.

Next, customers were asked to fill in a short form with their contact details, so they could receive their e-vouchers via email. Thanks to these efforts, of the 500 people who received an e-voucher during the eight-week campaign, 20% purchased from the company's online shop. Juanda explains, "Customers are not comfortable with a minimum purchase term when using e-vouchers. By removing this term, conversion rates skyrocketed to between 80% and 90%."

Reducing cancellation rates

Another common problem is that customers often do not go through with their purchases. In the case of DILI, around 40% of the company's customers "purchased" an item on its website but exited the site before making a payment.

Because the company's website captures data on all users, they know who made a purchase on the checkout page but didn't pay. So the company created an automated three-day cancellation system on its website for unpaid orders. The company's customer service team contacted clients in two stages, reminding them to pay.

Stage 1: After one day of not making a payment, customers are sent an email reminder.

Stage 2: After two days, the company called customers to remind them and ask if they experienced any issues when making a payment.

The implementation of this simple reminder system caused the cancellation rate to decrease massively, from 40% to 5% after two months, helping the company secure more paid orders. Based on this campaign, Juanda says that online customers still long for human interaction even when shopping online.

According to feedback, customers say that sometimes they forget to pay so these reminders help them finish the process. Some customers are afraid they will make mistakes when purchasing online but are unwilling to contact the company. So after speaking with the company's customer service team, they're more confident to make their online purchase.

Other customers are simply confused about how to make a payment, as they are new to online shopping.

Increasing customer loyalty in a competitive online market

In a super competitive online market like that of Indonesia's, local shoppers are spoilt for choice. This means that customer loyalty tends to be low for some brands. To deal with this, the DILI team came up with the #KetemuDamn (which translates to "MeetDamn") brand activation campaign. The team would reward people wearing the company's products in their daily activities by giving them e-vouchers.

Juanda says: "We often meet people wearing our products when we're out. However, we don't get a chance to thank them and appreciate their support. It's awkward if we just approach them and say thank you. Therefore, through this campaign and the continuation of the O2O e-voucher program, we hope to thank our loyal customers and build awareness for our online shop."

Digital buyership in the rest of Asia

It's important to look at digital buyership in the rest of Asia for comparison. Southeast Asia holds the world's quickest-growing internet market, with almost 3.8 million new users each month. As many consumers in Southeast Asia tend to not have easy access to physical stores, or have a smaller range of goods and services available to them, online shopping, or e-commerce, provides a solution.

A study by Google states that the region could achieve a $200 billion internet economy by 2025. In such a competitive e-commerce market, it's important to stand out from the other countless businesses that have moved online. If you're thus relying on your website for business, here are a few tips on what to give your visitors.

1. **An opportunity to speak with you** – This can come in the form of meetups, workshops, or webinars.
2. **Teasers** – Something that entices them to return to your website. For example, you can say something like "We have a new collection coming soon!" or "Keep an eye out for our promotions."
3. **Shareable content** – We scroll through blog posts, photographs, audio, and videos every day. Use them.
4. **Outlets for communication** – Make your email address and actual working phone numbers easily available and provide social channels for customer support.

There are so many tools available these days for you to track whether your efforts are paying off. Use them. To assess how your website's doing, make use of tools like website traffic analytics (e.g., unique visits), email subscribers, and inbound links. These key performance metrics are essential indicators of what you're doing right and what needs to be changed.

Key takeaway: Despite the growth of ecommerce, human interaction is still crucial. It also gives your brand personality and makes it more memorable.

4.4 Driving awareness and sales by combining online and offline experiences

If you only had a few weeks to launch your biggest product of the year, what would you do? New Balance managed to do this by partnering with one of Asia's biggest performing artists, Jay Chou.

Now, you might argue by saying that only a big brand could pull off such a thing, but essentially, their social media blitz campaign can be broken down into five simple steps that anyone can follow. By catering to local tastes and using the right platforms, you can actually achieve quick results in a short time.

Step 1: Create a product that your customers and the media will love

Mandopop superstar Jay Chou is a household name in many parts of Asia. Seeing the opportunity in this, New Balance partnered with PHANTACi to design 10 new exclusive shoes inspired by Chou's 10 previous albums.

Step 2: Give your audience just a taste

To maintain buzz around the product, the team at New Balance decided that the shoes should be released one by one over a month. New Balance China's former Marketing PR Manager Ann Chen says this is something that no other sports brand has ever done. She states, "Our biggest challenge though was how to make sure that the media is still interested when we launched, say, the fifth shoe. Also, considering that news stays on social media platforms like WeChat for less than five hours, how do we ensure that our news won't get easily replaced?"

Is playing hard to get good for business? Luxury brands can attest to this. Luxury marketing ultimately relies on positioning—that premium products provide greater value. Elusiveness creates the notion that the product is of a high standard and is worth the wait.

You might wonder how this relates to streetwear. Thanks to Instagram and younger shoppers favoring distinctive styles over craftsmanship, streetwear brands such as Supreme are quickly attaining the same status (and prices) as luxury brands.

Step 3: Make it exclusive

Some Chinese consumers love exclusive products. So to create an air of exclusivity for its new products, New Balance announced that the 10 special edition shoes were not for sale but for display only. Chen explains, "The display-only, not-for-sale shoes and all the stories we cooked around them lead to one aim: to launch the (for sale) limited edition New Balance x PHANTACi 997.5 in the middle of September."

This idea of exclusivity is not new, but brands that have made it big employ this strategy known as 'the drop.' Makeup mogul Kylie Jenner, for example, has used this to immense success. Huge buzz is built up around a new product prior to launch, and knowing that the item is being released in limited quantities makes it more exciting for customers to get their hands on it. Jenner's products consistently sell out within minutes of release because consumers are hyped up and ready to buy.

Step 4: Promote your product launch on social media

Chen explains, "By releasing one new product every two days, we maintained the hype among the media and consumers. We also used social media channels like WeChat, as it's the 'mainstream' media outlet in China at the moment." (WeChat is a mobile messaging app and is one of the leading social networks worldwide, with 1.4 million active users. Definitely not a bad platform to make use of.)

So how did New Balance use WeChat during the launch? Chen explains the team's three-pronged approach:

1. Make use of big WeChat accounts (or public accounts, as they are called in China). Chen says, "Just like what we did with media advertorials, we placed the WeChat stories in advance so that they'd be released based on our timeline."

2. Create an HTML5 campaign page. They worked with a media partner to create an H5 campaign, in order to figure out the 'most popular' model out of the 10 album shoes. This was done to drive as much attention and participation as possible within a short amount of time. So after 14 days, they could find out the 'top 3 favorites' among netizens.

3. New Balance's official WeChat. Chen explains, "We also promoted all our content on our official New Balance WeChat account simultaneously." She says that the publicity from WeChat accounts and WeChat influencers helped generate a tremendous amount of free publicity.

"The media basically asked us for scoops. They wanted to be the first to report because they wanted to use the hype to generate more traffic to their platforms," says Chen.

When asked if print media was a focus for the campaign, Chen replies, "Print was a supporting tool in this case. I placed most of my budget and time to drive WeChat content."

Once consumers were aware of the new products online, it was time to take the hype to the streets.

Step 5: Take the hype offline and go international

Chen explains, "We were aware that what made a shoe so popular in China was through the sneakerheads and sneaker outlets either in China or internationally. So our approach was to engage those in the 'inner circle' first." Hence, to maintain the same hype offline, the team partnered with retail stores that sneaker influencers and early adopters considered as the go-to places for sneakers in China.

One week before the official launch, the New Balance China PR team organized an event for influencers and consumers to see the shoes they had only seen in the media. According to Chen, this helped generate substantial buzz the next day and the following days through these tier-one influencers (sneakerheads and tastemakers), and essentially the buzz lingered until mid-September when the products were available for sale.

These pre-launch parties are becoming increasingly common as a means of marketing to the younger crowd. Thanks to social media, consumers can watch their favorite influencers having fun at an event in real time, through avenues such as Instagram Stories.

To build awareness for the product launch outside China, the team created stories for the internationally renowned sneaker media, HYPEBEAST. Chen explains her approach, "With a limited budget and time, I categorized media by tier so that some media would talk about the next model the morning after we released the information. Other media outlets provided 'previews' for the next shoe to debut, whereas a few outlets did a weekly recap. That way, it felt like every week in August, the NB 997.5 was a recurring topic."

The results?

In only seven weeks, the campaign achieved:

- 16 times ROI of the PR investment
- RMB15,376,618 equivalent ad value
- 46,000+ comments and 20,500+ retweets on social media

Key takeaway: If you want to have a successful brand or product launch, it's worth taking the time to plan out the pre-launch activities or how you'll build buzz beforehand. And while many marketers love the allure of online marketing, offline marketing still has its merits when connecting with audiences, especially if you have a physical product to showcase.

CHAPTER 5: SHAKE-UP
TAKE SMALL STEPS, NOT HUGE LEAPS

"The journey of a thousand miles begins with one step."

- Lao Tzu

Now that you understand how to build trust and relationships with your audience, as well as relate to them on a personal level, we're going to share how to differentiate your brand. In a land of cookie-cutter and imitation companies, how can you stand out from the pack?

To answer that question, we analyzed some of the most successful executives and organizations in the region to find out what makes them different. We arrived at one possible answer: their ability to Shake-up their industries.

As Steen Puggaard rightly points out, Western businesses tend to jump off the deep end when it comes to shaking up their space. Meanwhile, in Asia, he says that you need to take baby steps when it comes to disrupting the status quo. Why take baby steps? Because some executives in Asia have a lesser appetite for risk than their Western counterparts. If you want to get them on board with your plan, you'll need to showcase small wins on an ongoing basis, and showcase how it's all building up to your grander plan of shaking things up.

The caveat here is that we're not suggesting that you create some drastic new product or service in order to be successful. Sometimes all it takes is being able to look through the holes in the wall and identify the opportunities that lie between the gaps, as Puggaard puts it.

To give you an example, when I started my marketing and sales training business, I was initially discouraged by the slew of other training companies in the region. "How will I stand out?" I asked myself.

Then I started reviewing each of their curricula. Many of their training courses were based on a set curriculum—something they could use regardless of the company or industry. And while this works great if you're looking to scale a business, I realized I wanted to take a bespoke approach to training that incorporated my consulting background. Therefore, I'd first interview the heads of the company to identify the challenges and opportunities within the organization. Only then would I suggest a particular curriculum. This approach has helped me differentiate and grow my business in a saturated market.

You may be thinking, "Well that's not revolutionary, is it?" And you'd be absolutely right. As I mentioned earlier, the point of shaking things up is not to shake things up just for the sake of it. It's about identifying the holes in your industry's wall and figuring out how you can plug the gaps.

In this chapter, we highlight some successful leaders and organizations that have built their empires using their ability to shake things up.

5.1 Influencing public sector decision-makers

How did a small Singaporean startup achieve a readership of 1.1 million—in just a year and a half? The answer is simple: by knowing and understanding their audience. GovInsider provides a platform for government officials and public servants to learn from their peers and other experts in the field. In just two years, they managed to speak at United Nations summits and have even facilitated MOUs between governments. All of these while building an ever-growing audience of senior officials.

Gaining influence over some of the most important decision-makers in the world is no easy feat. GovInsider's achievements can largely be attributed to how they tailored their services to the needs and interests of their readers. This is important in the initial 'Consideration' stage, where a consumer is willing to consider your product and wants to learn more about it before committing to it. Joshua Chambers, the founder of GovInsider, provided his five-step strategy on how to capture and hold the interest of potential consumers.

1. Provide a new narrative

In the era of the internet, information overload is definitely an issue. How can an organization make their content stand out amongst millions of other similar pages and platforms? For GovInsider, the key to capturing the interest of government was to choose an angle or format that had never been used.

What was this unique angle? Chambers knew that people are interested in stories, especially those that haven't been told before. So GovInsider's first story touched on Beeline, Singapore's first crowd-sourced bus service platform. Chambers says, "The scheme had been covered by other press but hadn't made a huge impact due to the angle they chose."

So GovInsider went with something different. "We decided to write a long-form story that took thousands of words and focused on the people involved in the project as much as the outcome it would achieve," explains Chambers. It worked. The story reached 120,000 officials in just its first couple of days. Eventually, Singapore's Prime Minister, Lee Hsien Loong, shared the story on his Facebook page.

"People wanted to read something inspirational, and these lessons translate to many other projects," says Chambers. In particular, the cybersecurity industry is taking the wrong approach, he believes. "Often, their stories are about scaring people with the latest threats, but our analytics show that readers are tired of this. Instead, they want to learn new skills and see how other countries are implementing innovative new approaches," explains Chambers.

2. Entertain your reader and capture their attention

As consumer behavior reports tend to focus on common trends, it is easy to make the mistake of subscribing to stereotypes about consumers. GovInsider recognized that government marketing doesn't necessarily have to be too formal. Dreary reports full of bullet points and charts don't have to be the only means of disseminating information.

Government officials are the same as the rest of us, after all. "They want to be stimulated and entertained. They want to learn from heroes and read something simple and informative," says Chambers. He says that GovInsider's competition isn't from other marketing initiatives or publications—it's Facebook, Twitter, and YouTube.

If you think about it, it makes sense. Where do many people spend their free time online and occasionally (for better or worse) get their news from? Social networks like Facebook, Twitter, and YouTube.

3. Keep your headlines short and provocative

A common mistake is to use jargon when trying to appeal to potential consumers. Although it is important to remain industry-specific, the product should be presented in an educational manner that is tailored to the consumer. Chambers says, "There is too much unnecessary jargon when communicating with government." By keeping it short and sweet, you present the info more efficiently and in an easily digestible manner.

By this stage, you should know a bit more about your potential consumers. You can thus send them more targeted content that addresses their specific needs. This also shows your audience that you can provide the solution to their problems. GovInsider hence teaches its reporters to first summarize their stories in a single catchy headline. For a piece on Britain's government digital strategy, they went with the straightforward headline: "Why Britain

Banned Mobile Apps."

"This went viral and also made a big difference in Indonesia, where many city mayors were competing by setting targets to build new e-services. After reading the piece, they went back to the basics and looked at how to reform their processes instead," says Chambers.

4. Avoid a one-size-fits-all approach

In the case of GovInsider, their target readers, people in government, are never all the same. Readers in different countries and agencies have different interests and needs. Therefore, GovInsider's analytics help tailor stories to ensure that they are achieving impact. The startup tracks the keywords and angles that are most popular on a daily, weekly, and monthly basis, targeting areas where there is particular traction or interest.

As Chambers explained, in countries like Singapore, officials want to learn about global leaders—essentially, their peers in the field. However, developing countries often have a more inward focus, as they have local challenges to contend with most importantly. They would prefer something that relates directly to their own objectives.

5. Make your audience the hero, not you

This last point may be the most important. How can you inspire people and improve their lives? Organizations should keep this query in mind when crafting their messaging to potential consumers. The goal here is to nurture your audience with contextual or targeted content.

Working with the government, GovInsider was aware that "Officials are motivated by the public good," says Chambers. "They have dedicated their lives in the service of their country and their fellow citizens." Therefore, this is the angle GovInsider uses to reach out to a greater audience.

Making things easy is a secondary objective, but many organizations focus on this angle, rather than on the bigger picture. How does your initiative improve citizens' lives? What is inspirational or transformative about it? Organizations must remember this in the language that they use, the stories that they tell, and the outcomes they want to achieve.

Tech companies, for example, shouldn't talk about "IoT" or "cloud," Chambers says, because anything with these terms in the headline doesn't get read. Instead, they should talk about how they can help solve wicked policy problems or build predictive services. "Ultimately, our readers are our heroes," Chambers says. "We exist to serve them, and we obsess about it every day."

Key takeaway: Addressing your audience's personal concerns and seeking to nurture and inspire them is what will make them stick with you.

5.2 Uncovering and capitalizing on opportunities in the market

Although converting users is an important aspect of expanding sales, it doesn't address how to maintain consistent sales during off-peak seasons. Here's where companies have to differentiate themselves by coming up with innovative ways to engage existing customers. We spoke to the founders of Lully Selb, a streetwear brand for both modern and modest women, to find out how they did it.

According to the 2015-2016 State of the Global Islamic Economy Report, Muslim consumers spend an estimated $230 billion on clothing. That figure is projected to grow to $327 billion in 2019, surpassing the current combined clothing markets of the U.K. ($107 billion), Germany ($99 billion), and India ($96 billion).

More specifically, Muslim women spent $44 billion on modest wear, according to the report. Although the fashion dates back centuries, it has only recently become an emerging trend in Asia. The reason for this rise of modest wear in mainstream fashion most likely has to do with increased purchasing power and greater visibility of Muslim women globally.

What is Islamic modest wear exactly? It adheres to the Islamic style of dressing for women, which constitutes covering their heads, necks, arms, and legs. However, modest doesn't necessarily mean boring. Modern Muslimahs (Muslim women) don fashionable clothes and headgear that allow them to express themselves and their own personal styles.

With the industry booming, the Muslim clothing market is rife with opportunities. Big brands have already begun to venture into the industry. Italian luxury fashion house Dolce & Gabbana launched a collection of ankle-length dresses with matching embroidered head scarves and hijabs in 2016, and fitness brand Nike launched its first Pro Hijab line for Muslim women athletes in 2017. Other brands such as DKNY, Tommy Hilfiger, Zara, and Mango have also introduced collections of modest wear during Ramadan in recent years.

The strategy behind Lully Selb's success

So as a Muslimah, how can you look stylish while maintaining your Islamic values? That was the inspiration behind Lully Selb. Founded by two Singapore-based Muslimahs, Selma Bamadhaj and Nur Rulhuda, Lully Selb is shattering stereotypes of how a Muslimah should present herself without compromising her values.

However, retail has seen a decline in Singapore in recent years, with some shopping centers in the city's busiest shopping district, Orchard Road, only half full, even on weekends. Why then did the girls choose to start a Muslim fashion brand at such a risky time? Bamadhaj explains, "I was rather frustrated that most modest wear brands were too traditional looking, too feminine, too dainty, and overall lacking the aesthetics that I would wear."

Fed up with the lack of options, Bamadhaj hence decided to do something about it. She first broke into the fashion industry by sourcing fashionable and low-cost merchandise from Thailand and China and selling it via push carts and at flea markets. While she sold a few items that way, she realized she needed to take her brand online to grow its presence.

Helping fuel the interest in modest wear is the wide presence of social media in the region, with its visual format providing the opportunity for Muslim women to become more fashion-conscious and to express themselves through their choice of wardrobe. Like many fashion entrepreneurs, Bamadhaj turned to Instagram to build her community.

However, here's where Lully Selb makes a difference. While many brands pick influencers mainly based on their number of followers, Bamadhaj and Rulhuda wanted a more personal touch to the brand. Lully Selb selects unique individuals who are influencers in their own social circles. Although still considered influencers, they also act as unofficial brand ambassadors who will wear Lully Selb's clothing and accessories to get the word out about their brand.

"By featuring up-and-coming talent with a personality and style that suit our branding, a higher percentage of the influencer's followers liked our page as compared with the traditional bloggers we tried to engage. Some followers even asked where they could buy the shawl featured in her photo. So it was a big win for us in terms of brand awareness and incremental sales growth," says Bamadhaj.

Especially in such a niche market that doesn't receive nearly as much representation as it should, featuring smaller albeit still recognizable individuals makes the brand itself more accessible. As a result of their efforts, the brand once received a spike of over 400 Instagram followers within a few days, when an influencer posted a photo of her #ootd (outfit of the day).

More importantly, it adds a personal touch to an industry that seems to be losing its authenticity thanks to a saturation of Instagram influencers.

Continuing the conversation

Another way that Lully Selb personalizes their content is by sharing an inside look into their brand, from their textile design process to styling tips. This has led to higher engagement rates, as much as 40% higher than product- and sales-oriented content.

Bamadhaj explains one such instance: "Once, we posted a thought-provoking quote from a well-known Japanese designer and added a question in the caption to see how our fans would react. We were pleasantly surprised that it garnered an engagement level that was 50% higher than our average posts and proved to us that customers want to be part of our journey."

With all the focus on social media, it is easy to forget about an important digital channel that can and should still be leveraged: email. To keep their fans engaged on email, the duo sends newsletters to their subscribers once a week or once every fortnight. "We have an average open rate of 30%, which is around 9% higher than the average open rate for the retail industry. We've noticed that personalized subject lines like, 'We know you've been waiting for this!' have higher open rates compared with ones like 'New Product

Launch,'" says Bamadhaj.

However, a word of caution to those looking to break into niche markets: Religious practices and fashion don't necessarily go hand in hand. Although it has been proven that fashion can be successfully marketed to a Muslim demographic, a lot of research goes into it beforehand. Do your homework and take the time to understand your consumers before marketing to them.

Key takeaways: It's important to stay true to your brand and understand your audience. Advertising campaigns can alienate existing customers if they are inauthentic or trying to appeal to a market that is too wide. Also, equal effort has to be put into marketing to and engaging your current customers. Lastly, research is important. Niche markets are rife with opportunity, but sensitivities and consumer needs should be fully understood first.

5.3 Disrupting the South Asian dating scene

Many of us have tried dating apps at some point. For many busy young professionals, it's hard to resist the convenience of meeting a potential partner online. But for many South Asians, apps like Tinder "aren't addressing their desire to preserve their cultural and religious heritage," says KJ Dhaliwal and Sukhmeet Toor, founders of the dating app Dil Mil. The app aims to combine traditional South Asian values with modern technology.

Founded in 2014, Dil Mil offers a middle ground for South Asians who aren't looking for either hookups or arranged marriages. The app instead focuses on modern dating methods without downplaying religious and cultural identities. In contrast to arranged marriages, the power stays with eligible singles throughout the process of finding a partner.

Generating word of mouth by featuring success stories

Traditionally, "aunties," either actual family members or friends of the family, play the role of matchmaker in South Asian countries. But with Dil Mil, the matchmaking process is taking place on the app—kind of like a "virtual" auntie.

Dhaliwal and Toor worked together to build the app and website, and their hard work has paid off. Most of their user acquisition is organic. In other words, they gain users through non-paid avenues like word of mouth.

More recently though, they've been experimenting with video content. One of their videos, a satire about arranged marriages, has received 1.4 million views, showing just how strongly their content resonates with many youngsters. In addition, each week, Dil Mil releases a new video about one of their success stories across their social media channels, which has become a key part of the company's marketing and advertising.

Their marketing efforts paid off, as the duo raised nearly $4 million in pre-Series A funding and were backed by celebrity investors such as 500 Startups, Will Bunker of Match.com, and Scott Banister of PayPal. But what makes this app so different from the Tinders of the world?

Dil Mil is doing more than just bringing tech to cultural expectations, they're bringing predictive analytics and artificial intelligence (AI). The duo has built a learning algorithm that integrates dynamic rankings. Simply put, each time you log in, not only do you see relevant matches, but your prospects are also more accurately matched to you compared with your prior use. All you have to do is enter a few key details into the app, including your match preferences. From there, Dil Mil displays personalized matches for you.

Putting users in the driver's seat

If you're like many South Asians, you may be trying to find someone who meets both your and your family's expectations. However, putting your name up on dating sites can be problematic. Whether your parents are worried about you falling prey to hookup culture, or they simply cannot resist trying to "help" you improve your profile, you probably would prefer that they just didn't know about it.

That's where Dil Mil comes in. The founders learned from personal experience and observations that the current solutions on the market either couldn't cater to what South Asians were looking for, or were rampant with profiles run by the user's parents instead of the actual person. Dil Mil decided to solve this by giving full control to the owner of the profile. How?

You can only create a profile and log in through your Facebook account. This ensures that you're the only one with access to your account, thereby reassuring other users that they're not talking to someone's parents. In addition, only your first name is shown, which is again pulled from your Facebook account to ensure authenticity. You can see which mutual friends you have with a potential match. You also have the option of connecting your Instagram and LinkedIn accounts for further authentication. It's all up to you.

Dhaliwal and Toor realized that they could give South Asian singles what no other site could: the steering wheel. On the other hand, there are many apps that focus on the general population and families who want to make dating a "group experience."

Since launching, the app has been responsible for millions of matches and four marriages per week.

Key takeaway: Sometimes it's worth leveraging on your own personal experience to tailor a product or service to a niche demographic. It gives you an edge in addressing the needs of those looking for something different from the usual products.

5.4 Revolutionizing the travel industry by building a community

You're 40,000 feet above sea level, going 564 miles per hour, with 32 of the best minds from across Asia. Your goal? Revolutionize the travel tech industry. Is this even possible?

That's the question Hack Horizon co-founder and entrepreneur Kostadin Kolev asked when he organized the first travel tech hackathon on a plane from Hong Kong to London. (In six days, the Hack Horizon teaser video had 20,000 views and 200 shares, with only a $10 budget to promote the video.)

Why kickstart such a bold journey? Kolev, a 23-year-old from Bulgaria who lives between Hong Kong and London, explains, "It might be a Millennial thing, but travel is so ingrained in my life. And as an engineer, I saw too many opportunities to make the travel experience better, simpler, and more efficient."

As for his vision for Hack Horizon, "I joined forces with my co-founders, Kristy Hart and Johannes Jaeger, to galvanize the Asia-Pacific startup ecosystem, bring together top talent, and support them in building products that can help reshape the industry."

"Asia has moved beyond imitating the West and has developed into a home of world-class talent, innovation, and startups. Hack Horizon will not only put Hong Kong back on the map as a technology hub but also help break down the silos in the country's startup ecosystem," says Kolev. But creating a high-stakes, first-of-its-kind hackathon comes with some tremendous challenges.

"At the start, I spent months trying to get in touch with one of our current key partners. So after several months of no responses, I decided to take another approach and asked one of our advisors for an introduction. The next day, I received a phone call from an executive at the organization," says Kolev.

How did a 23-year-old secure deals with industry bigwigs twice his age? Kolev says that his young age started working in his favor once he started leveraging his insights as a Millennial in the travel industry. He also used this approach to secure speaking slots and eventually run his own Travel Tech events. Kolev admits, "Putting together something big that has never been done before, especially in your twenties, takes patience. You get so close to things about to happen and then they fall through. You have to wait for all the dominos to align."

Leverage content across multiple channels

Kolev knew that he had to first build a community of travel tech enthusiasts. His solution? Monthly travel tech meetups in Hong Kong and London called Travel Tech Tuesdays. By offering free events with quality content and discussions, Kolev brought his target audience together and set the agenda.

For those unable to attend Travel Tech Tuesdays, Kolev cast a wider net by creating Runway Rundown Reports. These reports offered insights into the latest tech developments in the airline industry. He hosted these reports on his website for download, as well as distributed them to top travel media. Eventually, executives at leading travel brands like Airbus, Cathay Pacific, AirAsia, and Marriott downloaded them. Once that happened, Kolev was able to reach out to them and begin building relationships much easier.

Through Travel Tech Tuesdays and Runway Rundown Reports, Kolev built a community of 4,000 travel and tech enthusiasts. Now that the community had been created, what exactly did Hack Horizon hope to achieve? Many could argue Hack Horizon is a PR stunt, but Kolev believes the travel industry needs a large public initiative to bring everyone together and showcase the potential of innovation through technology.

Key takeaway: If you have a great idea but lack the experience, focus on showcasing what fresh perspective you have to offer. Start with your vision and repackage your most valuable content into different formats to save you time and make it relevant to different audiences.

CHAPTER 6: TALENT

GROOM GENERALS, NOT SOLDIERS

"If you want to lift yourself up, lift up someone else."

– Booker T. Washington

Up to now, we've talked about the different marketing and sales strategies and tools available to grow your business in Asia. To take your business to the next level, however, you'll need to build your dream team.

I've been fortunate to work with some exceptionally smart and talented folks. My advice for building high-performing teams: Find people with the skills you inherently lack, train them rigorously, and empower them to do their job —without you.

In a previous role, I was responsible for managing marketing and growth for an agency. I developed the strategy and tried tirelessly to do everything myself, so I was doing everything from writing copy for the website to managing relationships with the media. I was trying to do so many things at once. That caused the whole initiative to move at a snail's pace.

My bosses would regularly check in with me regarding my progress, but I had little to show each time. I grew frustrated and knew if I kept at this pace, we'd eventually lose opportunities to our competitors.

Eventually, I realized I needed the right team to make my plan a reality.

Since I have little to no design skills, one of the first hires I made was an experienced designer. Next, I realized that I could write, but it was far more efficient to employ a copywriter who could handle the day-to-day writing tasks so I could look at the bigger picture. Finally, I hired someone with technical skills who could manage all of the software and platforms we were using at the time.

Seems pretty straightforward, right? Well, there was one catch. They were all based in a different country, with a three-hour time difference between us.

So, how do you manage a team that works remotely? It starts with training. I put every new hire through an extensive boot camp, on everything from how to write an email to content marketing best practices. If they pass the boot camp, then they continue working with me.

Through the boot camp, I'm able to see not only how they perform day-to-day tasks but also, more importantly, how they respond under pressure. This is important because as my former colleague used to say, "Working in Asia is like drinking from a firehose." It's true. Because the economy is growing so quickly, you have to be able to keep up with the market.

After several months, I had built a team that operated nearly autonomously. That, to me, has always been the true testament of a great leader—one who eventually makes themselves no longer needed.

Since hiring and building a team continues to be one of the biggest challenges for managers in Asia, we've spoken with some of the best leaders, and we've found out how they build and retain their top talent.

6.1 How to attract and retain top talent in Asia

Human resources is one of the most misunderstood and underappreciated functions in any organization. Many people think of HR as just posting job openings online. So how can HR move from an image of job posters to brand builders? As Chief Human Resources Officer at Singapore University of Technology and Design (SUTD) Jaclyn Lee, Ph.D. says, the answer is clever digital marketing.

We spoke with some successful HR practitioners who shared how they attract, engage, and retain top talent in Asia using digital marketing strategies.

Figuring out the best online channels to attract the talent you want

Many HR practitioners in Asia say one of their biggest challenges is attracting top talent, particularly in emerging markets. Understanding this gap in the region, Matt De Luca founded JobNet.com.mm, one of the fastest-growing job boards in Myanmar. Many local companies in Myanmar tend to rely on referrals or agencies to recruit employees. Matt, however, uses online platforms like Facebook Ads and Google AdWords for his clients.

Why Facebook Ads, you ask? Facebook is the most used digital channel in Myanmar. "This makes it the obvious choice to target users, particularly for employer branding purposes," says De Luca. It's also more cost-effective in emerging markets. He adds, "Running ads in Myanmar may be cheaper than in competitive markets like the U.S. For example, one could expect to spend between $350 and $600 in Myanmar."

Google AdWords, on the other hand, attracts candidates with the roles they're searching for. De Luca says, "For example, having a relevant landing page and choosing targeted ad keywords for the Burmese market, such as 'Sales Manager Yangon,' will naturally produce leads from candidates who are interested in working in Burma as sales professionals. This tends to result in better conversions and lower cost-per-clicks, ultimately reducing the cost-per-hire metric that HR pros monitor."

De Luca provides the example of how he and his team used Facebook and Google ads to attract candidates for a local beverage company. Across multiple digital channels, their ads reached more than 200,000 potential candidates, of which 6,000 translated into job views, and of which 250 became qualified applicants—or 1 qualified candidate per 800 ads run, at least in this example.
They also recorded 7,186 visits to their employer profile on JobNet, increasing company visibility. Even if applicants did not consider applying for a specific position, digital marketing can boost qualified applications for positions in the longer term by keeping the company's name on job seekers' radars.

Including a short video in your emails to keep candidates engaged

Now that you have caught the attention of top talent, how do keep them engaged with your brand? Adriano Corso, who managed digital recruitment across Asia Pacific at IBM Smarter Workforce, suggests taking a "recruitment marketing" approach. He explains, "HR pros must be able to engage their audience throughout the recruitment marketing funnel. And marketing automation tools such as email marketing play a key role in recruitment."

How can you improve your recruitment email click rates? Corso recommends including a short video and gamification aspect in your recruitment emails. "Results are incredibly high when a link to a short video, describing the company culture or the hiring process, is included in emails to qualified candidates, with click rates exceeding 50%. Moreover, conversion rates can easily go above 40% when real people are featured in the video or when a gamification aspect is included." Corso says that this approach is particularly effective with candidates in the tech or creative industries, as well as for senior roles in other industries.

Using analytics to retain top talent

So, you've managed to bring key talent onboard. Now, how do you ensure that they don't quit and join your competitors? Lee at SUTD says her team leverages analytics to improve employee retention. She explains, "Dashboards give us insights into employee demographics, growth trends, and attrition analysis. We are also able to deal with causation analysis to drill down into people issues."

For example, reviewing causation for turnover in critical and high-value positions is paramount, as failing to address root causes early can have a strong, negative impact on your organization's stability, productivity, and growth.

Lee explains: "In a study we conducted, we discovered that when our university campus shifted from the western to the eastern part of the island, turnover spiked.

Using analytics, we discovered that most of the employees who resigned lived in the western part of the island, which meant a long commute for them. The team then worked on recruiting talents living in the east and also providing transport options for those living in the west. As a result, turnover has been reduced substantially."

Although there are numerous ways to approach data collection, in this example, the university collected demographic information about its employees, including home address, commute time, nationality, and other key factors. Then this information was organized into an analytics dashboard, enabling the HR team to track causation in real-time.

Supercharging your HR efforts with digital marketing

Digital marketing can most definitely give your HR efforts new strength, helping you attract, engage, and retain top talent and build your company into a world-class employer brand.

Have you tried any of these digital marketing techniques in your HR activities? If so, it looks like you're more of a digital marketer than you thought!

Key takeaway: Instead of using traditional recruitment channels like headhunters, try leveraging your company's online channels to attract and nurture talent. As for capturing candidate's attention, videos can be a great way to stand out and add some personality to your recruitment efforts. Additionally, analytics are a great tool for finding out why people stay and why they go.

6.2 Cultivating a team that never quits

When you're starting a new business and the future of your company is unsure, how do you ensure that you retain the best people? In my 12-year career, I've been fortunate that no one has ever quit my team (at least for non-personal reasons, e.g., moved to a new location, started a family, and so on). I've learned a few things over the years about how to make sure you have the best team possible.

1. Tie each employee's personal goals to their professional ones

When someone joins my team, I ask them one question: "What are your goals or hobbies outside of the office?" Why ask this question? Remember that your staff have their own lives after work. It's important to find out what their interests are, so you can help them grow both personally and professionally. You'll have a better chance at motivating staff if you can align their personal goals with their professional ones.

For example, when I found out that one of my team members enjoyed writing, I worked with her to sharpen that skill and eventually introduced her to one of the top marketing media agencies in India. Now, she's one of their top contributors, and I couldn't be more proud of her.

It is unfortunately still quite common in Asia for some business environments to conform to the idea of staying late to show your commitment to the company. As a supervisor though, I'd be happier if my team finished their tasks during regular office hours. That's why I discourage my team from working long hours. How do I help them avoid that? If they're falling behind on a project, then we will discuss how to make the process more efficient so they can finish on time.

Also, make it mandatory for your team to research and learn more about what's happening in their space. That's why I ask everyone in my team to take an hour or two each week just to read educational materials relevant to their role. Every Friday, we'd set aside time to discuss our learning with the whole team. We also encourage staff to join and participate in relevant industry events, so they can learn from others' experiences too.

Explain to them that yes, it will help the company, but it will help them more in their long-term career.

2. Play to your team's personality types

You'll often be working with a variety of different personalities. That's why it's important to find out during onboarding what their preferences are. For example, do they like structure or free-styling it? If some staff prefer more hands-on guidance, then I will work closely with them. On the other hand, some prefer to work on their own. In that case, I'll only step in when they want me to.

Also, you have to let them fall and pick themselves back up. This one is tough for micromanagers. But if you want your team members to grow, you have to let them fail every once in a while. That's not to say you should allow them to fall behind on a regular basis, but occasionally, it's good for them, as they often learn more from the experience. That's why every week, my team would catch up and share a project or task that didn't go well. Then each person had to share what they learned from the experience and how they would improve the situation next time.

If you give your team the opportunity to reflect on their losses and identify the root cause, they'll be much more prepared the next time.

3. Maintain honesty if you want loyalty

Have your team's back, no matter what. A team is like a family. You may fight among yourselves, but no one outside the team should be able to attack you. Maybe it's the protective father in me, but I've always figured that bosses should protect their team members and be ready to fall on their sword. That means if you're leading a team and the team fails to meet their objective, own the responsibility and convey that to other stakeholders, if necessary.

Honesty is a two-way street. Can you take criticism or feedback from your employees? Your team members need to be comfortable enough to be honest with you. If they're not able to confide in you, how do you expect to maintain a strong working relationship with them?

That's why during every appraisal meeting with my team, I have them review my performance as a supervisor. I ask them point-blank: "What do you think I could improve on as a manager?" I won't let them off the hook until they provide at least one suggestion.

Don't like hearing about your weaknesses? Well, grow some thick skin or risk losing your staff.

Key takeaway: If you want to build trust among your team, create an environment where they feel safe to experiment and fail. By aligning each team member's interests and personalities with their actual work, you'll keep them motivated and more engaged in their role. Lastly, ask your team members to provide feedback for you as a leader. By hearing them out and hopefully acting on their feedback, you'll grow as a manager and they will respect you more.

6.3 Training and delegating to grow your organization

Asia's startup scene is booming. The success of companies like Grab, Lazada, and Zalora are a testament to the fact that the region is increasingly becoming a great place for establishing a startup. No surprise then, that so many people are using Asia as the base for their new ventures.

However, when you're starting from scratch, how do you ensure that you have a good team behind you to help you achieve your dreams? Rich Burns, founder of ROAS Media, is one of the individuals who took the plunge by building his own company. He shared with us the importance of having the right people and how to get the best talent.

Burns initially struggled to build a team. Having previously worked at Facebook, he was used to the "luxury of applicants flooding in from around the world." So his strategy was to promote the company's vision and plans for growth. Then, he learned how to pick out candidates who were genuinely excited by this vision and growth to date. More importantly, he identified candidates who were enthusiastic about his plans for the company.

How did he do this? He says, "Before sharing your vision with potential hires, ask your team what the company vision is. If the people who work with you every day can't clearly communicate this back to you, then chances are you won't do a good job communicating the vision to potential hires. Your vision for the company should be infectious. It should stir up the right candidates and fill them with ideas."

If you're not sure what your company's vision is in the first place, it's always a good idea to aim high. As Burns says, "Your company's mission should envision you shooting through the stratosphere. It should be so big and out-there that it has its own gravitational pull and naturally attracts the right people on this journey with you while you blaze a trail through the skies together and attract the attention of future team members. Your vision needs to be big enough to inspire awe and big enough to fit the dreams and aspirations of the people you hire, so that along the way to achieving this vision, they're achieving their goals and things they never even imagined possible."

Burns brings up an often overlooked point. He states that the worst thing about the hiring process is that there's no value for potential candidates—only the one candidate who gets the role. ROAS Media sought to change the hiring process by offering a training boot camp on the weekends to help candidates upskill and gain new insights. Skills taught include everything from how to write an effective email to managing and working with other team members. At the end of the boot camp, they could assess candidates on their current knowledge and skills they had absorbed from the session. This way, candidates would be on more level ground. Ultimately, those who weren't fortunate enough to receive a job offer still received valuable industry training.

Burns realized the importance of his employees' personal goals as well. He explains, "I like to ask candidates how they see themselves playing a role in our company to help achieve the vision—even if it would mean taking multiple roles. I want these candidates to leave with the idea that if they join the team, they could achieve things over the next few years."

Giving up control and knowing when to delegate

Like we mentioned earlier, it's important to try not to micromanage, as much as you're terrified that things will go wrong. Going from a one-man band to working in a team can be incredibly trying at first. Burns tells us some of the biggest issues he faced.

First, trust. Particularly with new clients and where a lot of money is involved. It's not easy telling someone that you've got it from here and that you're taking the driver's seat with their millions of dollars in ad spend. Burns says his best solution to this was to ask clients to trust them, but to just show them how they were right at the outset, and then they could talk about something more long term together. This is why they offered contracts that could be cancelled anytime within the first 30 days.

Second, saying no to deals that are worth more than your previous salary. Burns says he learned the hard way that people don't always want to hire you for your expertise, and sometimes they want to hire you just so you can help prove that their strategy is the right strategy. What they failed to mention is that eight other agencies before you had tried and failed with this same strategy. So, sometimes, you just have to say no.

On a more personal level, you may have to give up control of your own life in the early stages of your business. Many startup owners can probably relate to this. Burns speaks of how the 24/7 nature of a startup meant that he was constantly on call. He says, however, "Fortunately for me, my wife Laura had watched her dad go through the same journey when he started his business. In hindsight, it's a huge blessing, as you need a partner who is supportive of the midnight calls to U.S. clients, the 4 a.m. wakeups for Australian clients, and my biggest faux pas—taking my laptop to the movies just in case there was a 'fire' to be put out."

Burns knew, however, that there is no growth if you only rely on one person, i.e., yourself. A good team was required to lay the foundations for a solid structure. As he says, "By delegating to your team, you, as the organization's leader, can spend more time looking at the bigger picture. To do so though, you need to make sure that the team is properly trained and feels empowered to make decisions. That's why I put all my new recruits through the boot camp. If they pass the boot camp, then I have the confidence to let them take over the reins, at least for some parts of the business."

To make sure they feel empowered, Burns tells each of them to think as if they were running their own business within the organization. That means that they can make internal actions without necessarily consulting him. However, he makes sure to remind them that if they have any questions, he's still happy to provide guidance. Burns explains, "This way, I'm not a hindrance, and there's nothing more motivational than feeling like you're running your own business while still having a safety net in the form of a helpful manager."

If you can effectively train and delegate, it's a win-win for you and your team.

Key takeaway: The nature of business has changed, such that the workplace has evolved into a space for employee's personal growth as well. By knowing when to delegate as a manager, you can empower your employees to grow both professionally and personally. If you have a strong vision that aligns with their own goals, you can rest assured that your team will also be working for the best interests of the company.

6.4 Growing a team of all-stars by leading by example

Ever wondered what it takes to have a successful team? David Liu, Chairman at Weber Shandwick (China), knows a thing or two about growing an effective team. When Liu joined Weber China in 2000, it only had 20 employees. It now has around 380.

In 2003, Liu grew the business by over 90%. However, that year was also the most challenging year for him because the team was young and the workload was immense. So how did Liu take a young team and turn them into industry all-stars?

Don't be afraid to "lose face" among your employees

Liu feels that his status as a key opinion leader (KOL) has raised not only his own personal profile, but also the profile of Weber beyond the PR industry.

Liu also made multiple public appearances throughout his career and performed at the company's annual parties. For one of the annual parties, he appeared in drag as Wu Zetian, the only woman to rule as the emperor of China. In subsequent parties, he came as Marilyn Monroe, Hello Kitty, and Lady Gaga. That takes guts! And more importantly, it takes the ability to "lose face"—something many Asian executives couldn't bear doing.

I still remember meetings early in my career where I was terrified to speak up. Not necessarily because I was afraid of losing face but because I feared that any mistakes I said would unintentionally make my boss lose face. Therefore, I remained quiet and fed him any ideas and talking points I had beforehand. If he or she gave the green light, then I felt more confident in speaking my mind with prospects and clients.

In 2012, Liu's public popularity exploded after his appearance on a popular TV show called "You Got Hired." On the show, he was invited to be on a panel and give career guidance advice to job seekers. Since his first appearance in 2012, he continues to make regular appearances on that show, often taping four episodes over two days.

How does this translate into building relationships with your team though? By building his own personal brand, Liu has inspired others to follow in his footsteps—by creating an environment where staff can openly express themselves without the fear of "losing face."

Build a team of all-stars around you

We've already mentioned the importance of having a strong team. Liu also corroborates this and says that his staff play an important role in his professional success, especially because PR depends on teamwork. It's only possible for his firm to secure clients' trust when it has a solid team behind it. That's why Liu feels that one of his greatest achievements over the past 17 years at Weber has been finding, hiring, and retaining talent.

Liu says it's not easy forming the right team. There's an industry talent war. Liu says, "Startups to larger competitors both want your talent. Going forward, the staff at Weber will continue to play an important role, as the future will require people with skill sets in technology, research, and analytics."

Be the first one in the office and the last one out

In his early days at Weber, he was often the first one in the office and the last one out. It wasn't until around 2004 that Liu was able to focus on the macro direction of the company because by then, other senior execs had come onboard.

Key takeaway: Practice what you preach. If you want your team members to build their own personal brand, then do it first. If you want them to be dedicated and hard-working, make sure you're the hardest working person in the company. Remember, as a leader, you set the tone for the rest of the team.